FREE AND PUBLIC

Cartoon by R.B., from *Weekly Mail*, 28 June 1902 (by permission of Llyfrgell Genedlaethol Cymru/The National Library of Wales)

FREE AND PUBLIC

ANDREW CARNEGIE AND
THE LIBRARIES OF WALES

RALPH A. GRIFFITHS

UNIVERSITY OF WALES PRESS

www.uwp.co.uk

British Library Cataloguing-in-Publication Data
A catalogue record for this book is available from the British Library.

ISBN   978-1-78683-774-5
e-ISBN   978-1-78683-775-2

Photograph on chapter openers by philipp k. from FreeImages
Typeset by Chris Bell, cbdesign
Printed by CPI Antony Rowe, Melksham, United Kingdom

CONTENTS

Illustrations   vii

Abbreviations   ix

Preface   xi

1. The Public Library   1

2. Andrew Carnegie, 1835–1919   7

3. Philanthropy and the Free Library   11

4. Early Public Libraries in Wales   19

5. Andrew Carnegie and Wales   25

6. Creating Carnegie Libraries   33

7. Building the Carnegie Libraries of Wales   41
    Sites   43
    Architects and builders   52
    Architectural styles   54
    Inside the libraries   58
    Patrons   64

8. Abortive Proposals for Carnegie Libraries   71

9. The Carnegie Legacy in Wales   81

Notes   89

Gazetteer of Carnegie Libraries Built in Wales   105

List of Sources   141

Index   149

ILLUSTRATIONS

Map.   The Carnegie libraries of Wales   3

Figure 1.   Portrait of Andrew Carnegie   9

Figure 2.   Whitchurch library   37

Figure 3.   The entrance of Cathays library   38

Figure 4.   'Her turn next': Cardiff hopes for a Carnegie grant   42

Figure 5.   Penarth library   48

Figure 6.   Plaque at Treharris library   50

Figure 7.   Sculpture of Carnegie at Abergavenny library   57

Figures 8a, 8b.   Rooms at Cathays library   59

Figure 9.   The opening of Rhyl's library   65

Figure 10.   Plaque at Bangor library   67

Figure 11.   Margaret Carnegie visits Aberystwyth library   86

Figure 12.   Margaret Carnegie with the library committee
                inside Aberystwyth library   87

Figures 13–39.   Selected images of the Carnegie libraries of Wales   120*f*

ABBREVIATIONS

DWB   *Dictionary of Welsh Biography Down to 1940* (London, 1959), revised *https://biography.wales*

ODNB   *Oxford Dictionary of National Biography*, ed. H. C. G. Matthew (Oxford, 2004), and *http://www.oxforddnb.com*

RCAHMW Royal Commission on the Ancient and Historical Monuments of Wales

PREFACE

NDREW CARNEGIE, a Scots-American, was an industrial entrepreneur and philanthropist of titanic proportions. He was, too, an internationalist in his public career and in his personal life and beliefs. His philanthropy has had an impact across large parts of the globe and has had a particular impact in the United Kingdom, second only to that in the United States of America. An avid reader from an early age and himself a frequent writer, the value which Carnegie attached to the privacy of books and reading and the companionship of libraries led him to lavish a good deal of his wealth on the creation of free and public library buildings during the first decade of the twentieth century. More than thirty of these were built in Wales. Yet one is hard pressed to find a mention of Andrew Carnegie in popular and scholarly surveys of Wales's history that have been written in the past century. The explanation may partly lie in a preoccupation with identity and, recently, with 'Wales – a colony?' at the expense of the international context and reach of Wales's experience.

In recording and evaluating the Carnegie libraries in Wales, I have incurred a number of debts: at the beginning from the Royal Commissions on the Ancient and Historical Monuments of both Wales and Scotland, the librarians of the inter-library loan department of Swansea University, and the National Records of Scotland; and later from the staffs of a number of archives and records offices. It has been a pleasure to meet many of the dedicated people who today staff these libraries and patiently answered my questions (especially those at the Carnegie libraries of Aberystwyth, Bangor, Canton, Colwyn Bay, Newport, Rogerstone and Treharris). The National Library of Wales's 'Welsh Newspapers Online' (*https://newspapers.library.wales/*) has been invaluable as a resource, since local newspapers frequently reported Carnegie's letters to local authorities. I have been fortunate in the number of individuals who have encouraged the research and provided help on particular points, notably Neil Evans, Penny Icke, Bill Jones, John Law, Huw Owen, Maria Stanley, Roger Thomas and Chris Williams. Professor Williams generously offered to read an early draft of the text that follows, guiding me at a number of points in a field that is not normally on my radar.

At the final stages, I am particularly indebted to Penny Icke and Jon Dollery (who prepared the map) of the Royal Commission on the Ancient and Historical Monuments of Wales, and to Siân Chapman, Dafydd Jones, Llion Wigley and their colleagues at the University of Wales Press. And I am grateful to the Gwent County History Association for its contribution towards the costs of production of this book.

Swansea
Ralph A. Griffiths
November 2020

ONE

THE PUBLIC LIBRARY

What do we, as a nation, care about books? How much do you think we spend altogether on our libraries, public or private, as compared with what we spend on our horses?

John Ruskin, *Of Kings' Treasuries* (1865)

And a century later,

What we must try to see is that those who want to learn to read fully can do so and that they be allowed the critical space and freedom from competing noise in which to practise their passion.

George Steiner, *On Difficulty* (1978)

FREE PUBLIC libraries are at the heart of civil society in the United Kingdom and stand as witness to its quality. During the twentieth century they strove to bring knowledge, learning and leisure to the entire population, men, women and children, if more easily in towns and cities than in country districts – and they continue to do so. At the beginning of the century the challenge was to establish free public libraries from coast to coast and to sustain them by engaging the public that they were intended to serve. At the century's end, the challenge appears to have been to maintain the publicly funded countrywide library system which had emerged by mid-century to enrich 'the cultural fabric of communities', despite the consequences of two world wars.[1] This is as true of Wales as it is of the other countries of the United Kingdom.

Andrew Carnegie (1835–1919), the Scots-American industrial entrepreneur and philanthropist, was a pivotal figure during early stages of this saga, in England, Ireland, Scotland and Wales, and more broadly in the United States of America and elsewhere in the English-speaking world. His permanent legacy is represented by a considerable number of Carnegie Foundation Trusts, which continue to support cultural, educational and other causes, and, in Wales, by library buildings which remain part of the country's social, cultural, educational and architectural heritage.

THE CARNEGIE LIBRARIES OF WALES

The following list is arranged and numbered alphabetically. It is displayed on the map opposite according to the pre-1974 counties of Wales. The Gazeteer of Carnegie libraries later in the book is arranged similarly.

1. Abercanaid (Glamorgan)
2. Aberfan (Glamorgan)
3. Abergavenny (Monmouthshire)
4. Aberystwyth (Cardiganshire)
5. Bangor (Caernarfonshire)
6. Barry (Glamorgan)
7. Bridgend (Glamorgan)
8. Brynmawr (Breconshire)
9. Buckley (Flintshire)
10. Canton (Glamorgan)
11. Cathays (Glamorgan)
12. Church Village (Glamorgan)
13. Coedpoeth (Denbighshire)
14. Colwyn Bay (Denbighshire)
15. Criccieth (Caernarfonshire)
16. Deiniolen (Caernarfonshire)
17. Dolgellau (Merioneth)
18. Dowlais (Glamorgan)
19. Flint (Flintshire)
20. Llandrindod Wells (Radnorshire)
21. Llandudno (Caernarfonshire)
22. Merthyr Tydfil (Glamorgan)
23. Newport (Monmouthshire)
24. Penarth (Glamorgan)
25. Penydarren (Glamorgan)
26. Pontypool (Monmouthshire)
27. Rhyl (Flintshire)
28. Rogerstone (Monmouthshire)
29. Skewen (Glamorgan)
30. Tai-bach (Glamorgan)
31. Trecynon (Glamorgan)
32. Treharris (Glamorgan)
33. Troedyrhiw (Glamorgan)
34. Whitchurch (Glamorgan)
35. Wrexham (Denbighshire)

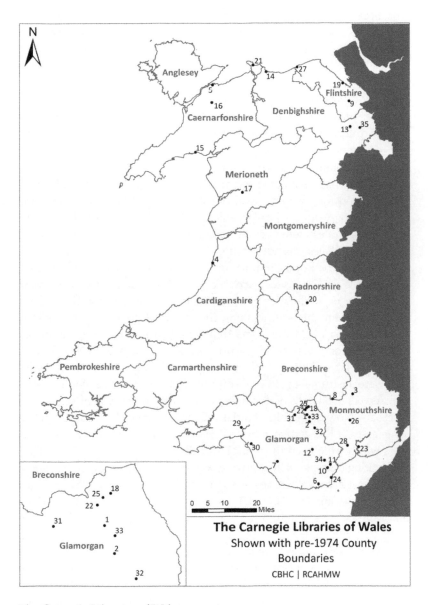

The Carnegie Libraries of Wales

Carnegie was a remarkably successful industrialist and steel-maker who became one of the world's most notable entrepreneurs and phi-lanthropists. He is judged to be 'the world's first modern philanthropist' and, according to his fellow billionaire J. P. Morgan, during his lifetime the world's richest man. In the winter of 2013–14 an exhibition held at the Scottish Parliament by the Carnegie Trust UK (in association with the Royal Commission on the Ancient and Historical Monuments of Scot-land) celebrated his international educational and cultural legacy. His native Scotland has been a handsome beneficiary of this legacy, but Carn-egie did not neglect Wales, especially in the way he helped to create public libraries in communities where few or none had existed before. Yet his Welsh legacy has been neglected, not least because the extent of his per-sonal support for library provision in Wales has not been fully identified and recorded. A proposal in December 2013 that his and the Trust's phi-lanthropy in Wales should be celebrated with an exhibition at the National Assembly for Wales was not pursued.[2]

However, the Royal Commission on the Ancient and Historical Mon-uments of Wales's website, *www.coflein.org.uk*, has begun to record some of the thirty or so libraries which were created as a result of generous gifts by Carnegie himself, totalling thousands of pounds, in the decade before the First World War – and that is aside from the grants he offered and which, for a variety of reasons, were not taken up. The Carnegie libraries of Wales helped to boost the public library movement in Wales and were instrumental in transforming the lives of the communities they served, in all parts of Wales from Dolgellau to Barry, from Tai-bach to Wrexham. Now that public libraries are facing financial difficulties and, in some cases, a less certain future, Carnegie's support for towns and par-ishes which were keen to sponsor free libraries for the general public is an inspiring example of how private wealth can be set to the public good.

Some Carnegie libraries – such as the buildings at Abergavenny (opened in 1906), Bangor (1907) and Treharris (1909) – continue to func-tion as libraries, engaging the public and inspiring pride in those who work in them. A few are neglected (including Aberystwyth's library, opened in 1906), and yet others have been strikingly refurbished by their local authorities (as at Colwyn Bay (1905) and Cathays, Cardiff (1907)), or are now given over to other public community purposes (as in Brynmawr (1905) and Bridgend (1907)). Only a very small number have been either disposed of (such as the small library at Troedyrhiw) or demolished (as in Abercanaid (1903)).

Like church and chapel buildings in Wales, the Carnegie libraries were built close to the heart of their communities, acting as community centres and meeting places or else, more fundamentally, as freely available havens for quiet contemplation and self-improvement. Today, when the professional public librarian seems to be about to join the ranks of endangered species, the local librarian and their (usually volunteer) assistants who staff these libraries are the successors of those librarians who have been able over the past century and more to place their specialist knowledge at the disposal of young readers as well as adult men and women, the poor and the better-off – in short, 'the public' – and whose skills and experience introduced others to reading for the first time and thereby changed lives, deploying what has been identified as their 'capacity for empathy'. Simon Jenkins, writer, architectural historian and chronicler of our own times, has described the potential role of the library well:

> Libraries and churches have a shared metaphysic. [Libraries] embody the cultural identity of a place as its archive, museum and collective memory . . . The Victorian tycoon Andrew Carnegie, first great patron of public libraries in Britain and America, dreamed of one in every town and village. His vision awaits renaissance.[3]

With an even broader social and cultural agendum in mind, the novelist and playwright Irvine Welsh, like Carnegie a patriotic Scot who relocated to America, recently wrote in the free weekly magazine the *Big Issue* about libraries, alongside independent bookstores, as 'these little boot-camps of interaction where people can go'.[4]

TWO

ANDREW CARNEGIE, 1835–1919

NDREW CARNEGIE was born into a poor household in the town of Dunfermline in Fife. His father was a humble handloom linen weaver by trade and a nonconformist in religion, with Chartist sympathies. Depression in the domestic linen industry caused the family to leave for America in 1848, moving to the Pittsburgh area where relatives had already settled some years before. As the elder of two sons, at the age of thirteen Andy (as he was known) took a job as a bobbin-boy in a local cotton factory. The sheer energy and thirst for knowledge which he displayed then and throughout his life attracted the attention of several employers in these early years. He soon became a messenger-boy at the O'Reilly Telegraph Company in Pittsburgh in 1850, and then, three years later, clerk and telegraph operator for Thomas Scott, the assistant superintendent of the Pennsylvania Railroad Company. This was a crucial step because Scott took a liking to the youngster and recognized his ability to master detail and his incipient talent for effective management. Scott encouraged him to buy shares in railroad companies and, at the age of twenty-four, Carnegie succeeded Scott as superintendent of the western division of the Pennsylvania Railroad Company. By shrewd investments in building telegraph lines, bridges and locomotives and in oil, he not only supported himself and his family but by 1868 was able to move to New York a wealthy man. To the casual observer, Andrew Carnegie may have seemed an unimpressive figure – just five feet two inches in height and with a boyish face, which he sought to conceal by growing a fashionable beard that was kept in good trim for the rest of his life.[1]

Carnegie threw himself with enthusiasm and inventiveness into the iron and steel industry and its applications, especially following a visit in 1872 to Britain where he observed the new Bessemer steel-making converter process at work. In 1884 he formed a close association with the coal owner Henry Clay Frick, the so-called 'Coke King of Pennsylvania', who became chairman of Carnegie Bros and Co. Carnegie was a shrewd, competitive and ruthless employer for whom the control of costs was paramount, even at the expense of employees' wages and amicable relations with the unions. As a result, there was a major shutdown of his works in Pennsylvania in 1892 and at Homestead an ugly strike that tarnished his reputation. But Carnegie and his partners survived the Great Depression of the 1890s, so that by the end of the century he had amassed one of the greatest personal fortunes that the industrialized world had ever seen: his share from his interest in United States Steel Corporation (as his firm had become) was put at $447 million.[2]

Carnegie often returned to Scotland even when he was a busy industrialist, and in 1897–8, three years before he sold his main interests in steel production, he bought the 30,000-acre Skibo estate in Sutherland and spent lavishly on rebuilding its castle in the neo-Gothic style. Thereafter, he and his wife, Louise Whitfield (1857–1946), the daughter of a prosperous New York merchant, whom he had married in 1887, spent most of their summers in Scotland, enabling them to entertain influential political and educational acquaintances, and to travel widely in Britain and beyond. It was at Skibo, as well as at his new mansion in New York on East 91st Street, that he and his private secretary, James Bertram, organized his philanthropic operations and conducted a vast correspondence with applicants for grants. Andrew Carnegie died at his country mansion, Shadowbrook, in the town of Lenox in western Massachusetts, on 11 August 1919.[3]

Figure 1. This portrait of Andrew Carnegie, by an unidentified artist *c.*1905, was gifted to the Smithsonian Institution by his daughter, Margaret Carnegie Miller, in 1974 (National Portrait Gallery, Smithsonian Institution, Washington: Creative Commons Zero (CC0) license 1.0).

THREE

PHILANTHROPY AND THE FREE LIBRARY

ANDREW CARNEGIE was not the first to sponsor free public libraries in Wales, the United Kingdom and the United States. In Great Britain and Ireland he was able to further his ambition within a context set by several Public Libraries Acts passed by parliament from 1850 onwards. These gave powers to a broadening range of local authorities in the second half of the nineteenth century to establish free libraries and museums. Despite some persistent opposition, boroughs, then towns, and then parishes were empowered to levy a halfpenny and then a penny rate for this purpose, provided they secured a measure of democratic endorsement. This was a major step beyond the earlier creation of privately endowed and subscription libraries. Scepticism lingered in a number of quarters, and the ambition of some small towns and parishes to have their own libraries out-ran the ability of their populations to raise sufficient funds from the rates, hence the need for philanthropy to support the public library movement almost from its beginnings. The present-day dilemma for local authorities as the democratic and accountable bodies responsible for public libraries is not new. Whilst still in his forties, Andrew Carnegie resolved to help.

Carnegie was a visionary, and rare among the wealthy entrepreneurs of his day – and for long after. His philanthropy was not directly linked to his own business interests or to his family, and his countless benefactions were made throughout much of his career, not simply towards its end.

His gift-giving, especially in the United States of America, gathered speed during the 1880s and 1890s when he was still an active businessman and entrepreneur. Moreover, he formulated a personal philosophy of philanthropy which he publicized in his writings. Among his prolific writings on industrial, economic and political issues are two essays written in 1889 on 'Wealth' and 'Best Fields for Philanthropy', which were first published in the *North American Review*. His extraordinarily influential essay on 'Wealth' was reprinted many times and with the more elevated title, 'Gospel of Wealth'.[1]

In this essay, he wrestled with questions of the social and economic purposes of wealth, how it should be deployed by those who possess it, and the social equality that it could and should promote. For, like a number of fellow prominent businessmen, he had a fundamental belief in political and social equality allied to equality of opportunity.

> The problem of our age [he wrote] is the proper administration of wealth, that the ties of brotherhood may still bind together the rich and poor in harmonious relationship.
>
> . . .
>
> What is the proper mode of administering wealth after the laws upon which civilization is founded have thrown it into the hands of the few?
>
> . . .
>
> There remains, then, only one mode of using great fortunes; but in this we have the true antidote for the temporary unequal distribution of wealth, the reconciliation of the rich and the poor.

For Carnegie, charity was not an end in itself, but rather it should 'help those who will help themselves . . . to assist, but rarely or never to do all'; neither should giving be 'impulsive and injurious'. Drawing on his own life and experiences, his conclusion was, for him, inescapable: among 'the best uses to which a millionaire can devote the surplus of which he should regard himself as only the trustee' is a 'free library . . . provided the community will accept and maintain it as a public institution'. As for the wealthy , his verdict is famous: 'The man who dies thus rich dies disgraced'. In a later essay, in 1891, 'The Advantages of Poverty', Carnegie went so far as to declare that 'There is really no true charity except that which will help others to help themselves, and place within the reach of the aspiring the means to climb'.[2]

His ideas and declared intentions were popularly admired, in Wales as elsewhere, especially in places which were in receipt of his benefactions. In the industrial port of Barry in south Wales, to which he granted the large sum of £8,000 for a new library in 1902, the Christmas eisteddfod held at the Welsh Congregational Chapel in dockland awarded the main prize for extravagant verses on 'Carnegie' that rose to biblical hyperbole:

An influence for good, a mighty power
Is wealth in hands that know its real worth.
Who hold their riches not as fortune's dower,
But held in trust for Him who rules the earth.
Who seek not acclamation or reward,
But simply follow the Divine command,
And, as a faithful steward of the Lord's,
Dispense His bounty with a lavish hand;
Which is the man whose name a household word
Is now where'er the English tongue is heard.

No sporting millionaire is he, who fain
Would crown an empty head with wreath of bay,
By yacht or horse's speed would fame attain.
And thus become the hero of a day;
Which fleeting laurels charm him not, he dreams
Of something nobler, something greater far,
With wealth and wisdom, both to aid his schemes.
Nothing terrestrial their success mar.
Wealth, wisdom, generosity, all three
Are central in the name of Carnegie.

A self-made man and well-made too is he.
An object lesson ne'er to be effaced
This is his motto, borne out faithfully –
'A man who dies rich is a man disgraced'.
Self-taught, he knows what aid a student finds in books;
And therefore, he, throughout the land
Brings the best thoughts of all the master-minds
Within the reach of every working-man.
Look where he will, the worker will ne'er see
A truer friend than Andrew Carnegie.

He never will need an epitaph,
Carved in fair marble, gleaming as the morn,
His name undestroyed by time,
On lips of generations yet unborn.
We may not pierce the future, dare not try
To raise the veil that hides from our ken,
 But this we know, that Christ will not deny
A man who truly helped his fellow-men;
And He who died for men on Calvary
Will find meet reward for Carnegie.[3]

In other quarters, however, his mode of philanthropy was interpreted as straightforward charity. This reaction was stiffened in Llandrindod Wells in November 1903. The Public Libraries Act had been adopted by the local council in 1902 and an appeal was made to Carnegie for a grant to build a new library. When his reply arrived it pointed out that the revenue from the penny rate would be insufficient to maintain such a library. The chairman of the council, James Edwards, evidently took umbrage. He was reported as having declared that 'he was not sorry to hear this letter read, as the town had hitherto got on without the aid of charity. They could do without Mr Carnegie's money.' When other councillors deplored his comments, the chairman stubbornly repeated them for the record. It would be another three years before a further appeal was made to Carnegie, and then, along with an offer of £1,500, James Bertram, Carnegie's secretary, took the precaution of requesting an assurance from the council that it would raise at least £100 a year from the rates to sustain the new library. The council accepted the grant – and the conditions that came with it.[4]

Carnegie's particular concept of what has been described as 'entrepreneurial philanthropy' was controversial in the business and industrial worlds of his own day and it has continued to be so ever since. Some regarded his distinctive form of philanthropy as a means of advancing his own interests and salving his own conscience, while the popular identification of 'Robber Barons' counted Carnegie as a prime example of the genre both before and after his death. There was an echo of this attitude in the major iron, steel and tinplate town of Llanelli when a proposal was made in 1914 that the borough should apply to Andrew Carnegie for help in building a new library. After a lengthy discussion, a spirited objection from Alderman Nathan Griffiths eventually carried the day:

There are many ways of doing penance, some people do so by contributing to chapels and churches, others by giving away to charities and charitable institutions: but I object on principle as a working man to making this application . . . I would not be a party to accepting a single penny piece of Carnegie's money. I have not forgotten the shooting of the strikers [at Homestead, Pennsylvania] by Pinkerton's men. Nor I would not touch a single penny of the money of the man who employed mercenaries to shoot down my fellow-workers. I may be on the side of the minority in the town, but I have a conscience.[5]

On the other hand, his essay on 'Wealth' had impressed the British statesman and Liberal prime minister W. E. Gladstone, who commended it to others in a review in 1890. Carnegie's writings on gift-giving, especially 'The Gospel of Wealth', are still fundamental texts of today's philanthropic movement on the accumulation of wealth and how it can then be put to work: a century on, it is said that the billionaire entrepreneur Warren E. Buffett recommended that the young Bill Gates might still read it with profit.[6] So long as great inequalities of personal wealth exist, so too will the purposes of its accumulation and the nature and motives of its disposition attract controversy.[7]

Carnegie sought to square the apparent contradictions in his philosophy by maintaining that the wealthy are but trustees for their poorer yet ambitious fellows. With more than a hint of (perhaps justifiable) vanity, later on in life he boasted that 'I do not wish to be remembered for what I have given, but for that which I have persuaded others to give'.[8] In 'Best Fields for Philanthropy', he expressed his views in particular on what he called 'free libraries'.

The result of my own study of the question, what is the best gift that can be given to a community? is that a free library occupies the first place, provided that the community will accept and maintain it as a public institution, as much a part of the city property as its public schools, and indeed, an adjunct to these. It is no doubt possible that my own personal experience may have led me to value a free library beyond all other forms of beneficence.

He recalled Col. James Anderson of Allegheny, Pennsylvania, who, when Carnegie was a teenager, made his personal collection of about 400 books available to young people in Pittsburgh on Saturday afternoons, allowing them to borrow from it as a veritable 'lending library'.[9]

He believed, further, that if it were possible, a free library should also be associated with an art gallery and museum, with a hall for instruction and lectures, though he was later to prove more cautious lest the funds made available were dissipated to the detriment of the core library itself. For Carnegie, 'A library outranks any other one thing a community can do to benefit its people. It is a never failing spring in the desert.' [10]

Carnegie's philanthropic expenditure was focused from an early stage, and most notably, on helping to make libraries available to the general public. An avid reader himself, he loved books and maintained a library in each of his main residences, in New York and, later, in Scotland. An inveterate traveller, his excursions in North America, Europe and elsewhere were as much educational as for business and recreation. His first grant for a public library was made to his family's home town of Dunfermline in Fife in 1879 when he was forty-four; his mother laid the foundation stone in 1881 during one of the summer visits which the Carnegies made to Scotland. His conception of philanthropy stemmed not only from his accumulated wealth and the obligations and opportunities which he believed stemmed from it, but also – perhaps more so – from his Scottish background and his restless energy as a self-made man. Dunfermline and Scotland were to benefit prodigiously. Significantly for the future, that first grant was made on condition that the town corporation of Dunfermline agreed to support the new library once it had been built.[11]

A similar condition was attached to his offer in 1881 to build a public library at the heart of his industrial 'empire', Pittsburgh. At first the offer was rejected, and only when the city authorities acquired the requisite powers to maintain a public library – something which authorities in the United Kingdom had been able to do since 1850 – did Carnegie renew the offer in 1889. It was quickly followed, in 1890 by a £90,000 gift to build a new public library in Edinburgh.[12]

In sum, by the beginning of the First World War Carnegie had enabled the building of no fewer than 2,811 library buildings in the United States and the British Empire, aside from offers to do so which were not taken up.

FOUR

EARLY PUBLIC LIBRARIES IN WALES

THE PRE-HISTORY of free, public libraries available to all is a centuries-long story of collections of manuscripts and books assembled by private individuals, organizations and institutions for the use of particular groups or members, and usually maintained by private wealth or subscriptions. Their number and value as reservoirs of knowledge and wisdom grew during the seventeenth and eighteenth centuries in Great Britain, including Wales, and, within their limitations, sometimes were made accessible to broader sectors of society, especially in towns and cities. In Wales, several parochial libraries were endowed from the eighteenth century onwards; they were mainly clerical in complexion. About the same time, subscription libraries of various sorts began to appear which might be more secular in tone, mirroring the extension of literacy: for example, reading or book clubs which might circulate from place to place in localities, most notably in tourist or spa towns; literary and scientific societies, especially for the middle classes; and mechanics' institutions and miners' and other workmen's libraries. These were available to their members or subscribers and, although they might sometimes be open to all social classes and female readers too, many were dominated by the middling sort.[1]

It was the hard-fought legislation of parliament in the second half of the nineteenth century that brought the free library potentially within reach of the general public in the United Kingdom, and at the same time posed daunting challenges of how such an ambitious aspiration could be made practical. This is the context in which Andrew Carnegie's remarkable vision fits.

Several Public Libraries Acts in the later nineteenth century, from the first in 1850, enabled urban, parish and, from 1919, county authorities in the United Kingdom to establish free public library services to be maintained from the universal rates. They placed the responsibility for adopting the Acts on local administrations democratically authorized. The first Act in 1850 set the rate at one halfpenny for libraries, to be raised to one penny in 1855, when its application was broadened beyond boroughs and towns. Manchester was the first authority to adopt the Act, in 1852. In Wales, Cardiff was the first authority to resolve to do so, in 1861.[2]

At some time or another, between the first Public Libraries Act of 1850 and the end of the century, most urban centres and parishes were considering whether or not to establish some sort of public library, supported by ratepayers and available to the population at large. From Cardiff, Swansea and Newport to Caernarfon, Blaenau Ffestiniog and Llanberis, such proposals were considered fitfully in Wales from the 1860s onwards, in some cases sponsored by an existing mechanics' institute or a literary and philosophical society, as at Newport, Pontypridd and Dolgellau. As an example, Pontypridd had a literary institute from 1860 which was replaced and absorbed by a new free, public library service in 1887; the library opened in 1889 but had to rely mainly on donations of books, newspapers and magazines in its early years.[3]

Another example was at Llanelli, whose mechanics' institute, founded in 1840, was joined by the Athenaeum seventeen years later, each intended for its members. The Public Libraries Act was adopted in 1897, and the property and substantial collection of books were duly handed over to the new, majestic public library, which opened in 1898 and had a hall for lectures and concerts, and a geological museum presented by the earl of Cawdor of Golden Grove, a major Carmarthenshire landowner.[4] Queen Victoria's Diamond Jubilee in 1897 was indeed the occasion of several proposals for new libraries, in Wales (in Brecon for example) as in the rest of the kingdom.

In other places, there was resistance – often fierce resistance – from reluctant ratepayers or from burgesses nervous of the potential costs involved in establishing and maintaining a public institution – as happened, initially, at Cardiff, Swansea, Merthyr Tydfil and Llandudno. At yet other places, no progress was made before the twentieth century, even where the

Acts had been adopted locally, as was the experience at Newcastle Emlyn, Broughton and Ogmore. Elsewhere, modest reading rooms were opened but, as at Kenfig, these did not extend their services to become libraries, whereas others were enabled to develop as lending and reference libraries too, as happened at Cardiff, Newport, Blaenau Ffestiniog and Holyhead. In short, it was a disparate and fragmented movement that depended on local attitudes as well as democratic practice. The creation of a public library also encountered practical obstacles that were related less to support for, or scepticism of, local aspirations to fund a free and public institution, than to the costs of maintaining such facilities in relatively small or poor communities, even when they were proposed for the suburbs of larger conurbations.

Public libraries were slow to appear in the south Wales valleys, where many coal-mining communities, large and small, established their own miners' institutes and welfare halls in the 1880s and 1890s; these included small libraries. They valued their independence from the public library movement supported by the penny rate, which would have been payable in addition to members' subscriptions, and from those public libraries later supported by Andrew Carnegie.[5]

While several library buildings in the larger towns of Wales – such as Cardiff and Swansea – were in the forefront of library architecture as it developed in the later nineteenth century, public libraries in smaller communities and towns usually had to lease quite modest accommodation in houses or other premises, or be placed in the corners of town halls and other public buildings (if there were any to hand). Carnegie's donations changed all that: his libraries were visually prominent, striking in style and centrally sited.

In the decades after 1850, the costs involved in acquiring books, newspapers and magazines were a major headache for communities, the revenue from the rates notwithstanding; in fact, the Acts discouraged the use of the penny rate to purchase books. Several libraries, especially those that had been preceded by private institutions or organizations, were fortunate to receive existing collections, as were the libraries at Pontypridd and Llanelli. At Llanberis the village library was taken over by a public library after the Public Libraries Act was adopted in 1895, and a number of books were donated to Aberystwyth's public library by the local literary society. At the larger industrial towns of Neath, Llanelli and Bridgend, the local mechanics' institutes transferred their books and furniture to the newer public libraries. Nor were private donations of books unusual: for example, Swansea's library benefited from several collections gifted by local worthies, and Aberystwyth acquired a collection of paintings – though this was subsequently mismanaged, so that a number of the paintings were 'lost'. At Beaumaris, Miss Allen's gift to the new library in 1897 was widely appreciated in the town, and the library itself came to be proudly known as the 'Allen Free Library'. At the other extreme, a proposal that the Powysland Club should transfer its museum and library to Welshpool borough council was defeated in 1887, and the library of the Royal Institution of South Wales at Swansea, founded in 1837, has jealously guarded its independence into the twenty-first century, albeit having been forced into disposing of many of its volumes along the way.

In some communities, local philanthropic patrons aided the creation of public libraries. At Bangor in 1870, Captain John Jones and Lord Penrhyn offered the town a combined museum and library, which was given an enthusiastic welcome when it opened the following year; but 'Jones's Free Library' soon proved too small to cater for the demands placed upon it by the townspeople. At Halkyn, the duke of Westminster, a major local landowner, offered a site for a village hall and library in 1896; this was well received by a poll of the inhabitants, and a newsroom opened two years later.[6]

Such varied responses to the Public Libraries Acts were significant and yet somewhat haphazard in the long-term perspective of the development of the public library movement. As at Barry and Aberystwyth, to take two examples, small public libraries were in rented accommodation and moved from building to building from time to time. At Aberystwyth, the public library had a peripatetic existence: previously lodged in Pier Street on a short lease, its first books were presented by the town's literary institute; the public library then moved to the Assembly Rooms, not far away in Laura Place, and in September 1903 it returned to former bank premises in Pier Street on a fourteen-year-lease, just before negotiations began with Andrew Carnegie for a purpose-built and permanent library building.[7]

In Barry, where the Public Libraries Act was adopted by a town meeting in 1891, a free reading room opened later that year adjacent to a small lending library of 'carefully selected literature' in leased premises in Holton Road. The library moved to larger premises in two rooms in the same road two years later, and there union and other public meetings were also held. Soon afterwards, as many as two houses were leased for the reading and lending libraries before, in 1902, an appeal was made to Andrew Carnegie to gift a permanent building appropriate for the growing port.[8] Such a state of affairs threatened libraries' continuity and left little money available from the penny rate, beyond the leasing and maintenance of buildings, for the purchase of books and newspapers, still less for the hiring of librarians.[9]

Andrew Carnegie transformed this situation, in Wales as elsewhere in the United Kingdom, at the outset of the new century, after he had sold his huge steel-making interests in 1901 and concentrated on philanthropy. As far as public libraries were concerned, he understood the difficulties encountered by local communities in wishing to implement the Public Libraries Acts. The experience of Abergavenny in 1901–2 plays a spotlight on the need for a public library, the difficulties of providing books out of the rates, and the opportunities presented by Carnegie's munificence. Although the borough was relatively slow to adopt the Public Libraries Act, on 8 October 1901 it opened a free library 'as an experiment'. The free library committee was bowled over by the response. Its first annual report on 24 November 1902 judged the library – which could not yet afford to be a lending library – to be 'an unqualified success': attendance in the reading room was sustained every week during the winter and summer months by 'a class of people representing all sections of society'; in one week alone as many as 1,500 were counted in, 270 of them 'ladies'. Moreover, their behaviour was 'exemplary'. It was clear to the committee that the library needed a permanent home and could sustain one. The borough council accordingly decided on 2 October 1902 to approach Andrew Carnegie. His secretary replied from New York on 30 December offering £2,000 to fund a new purpose-built library, on the understanding that (as the council assured him) a site would be made available and the rate assessment of the borough would amount to £110 per annum to support the library's activities. The council accepted these conditions without demur (as far as is known).[10]

The number of free public libraries built with Carnegie's grants during his lifetime is astonishing. They were almost exclusively confined to the United States of America and countries of the British Empire: 1,946 in the United States alone, 660 in the United Kingdom, 156 in Canada, 23 in New Zealand, 13 in South Africa, 6 in the British West Indies, 4 in Australia, and 1 each in the Seychelles, Mauritius and Fiji. The total number of 2,811 amounted to an expenditure of $50,364,808; the cost of building the 660 in Great Britain and Ireland was $15 million. And that tally does not take into account the substantial number of grants offered but not taken up. Nor does it include his grants worldwide for the purchase of organs – a total of 7,689 – for churches and chapels, including in Wales. The number of letters sent to Carnegie seeking grants from his seemingly inexhaustible resources after he had disposed of his interest in the United States Steel Corporation in 1901 is said to have seldom fallen below 400 a day; a goodly number of them arrived from Wales.[11]

FIVE

ANDREW CARNEGIE AND WALES

LTHOUGH CARNEGIE much preferred American democracy to the British system of government, there is no doubting the warmth of his feelings towards Great Britain and Ireland. His relationship with his native Scotland remained especially close throughout his life, but at several stages he developed intimate connections with Wales – as he did with the rest of the United Kingdom – and on several levels, industrial, political and cultural. When a letter arrived from Merthyr Tydfil in 1902 seeking funds for the building of a new library in the town, it seems to have been considered by Carnegie himself as well as by his secretary, James Bertram. The international significance of Merthyr's nineteenth-century industrial development may have prompted Carnegie (as reported by Bertram) to recall how important his Welsh workers had been in his iron and steel enterprises in Pennsylvania. In particular, he recalled how much he owed to the engineering genius of Captain William ('Bill') Richard Jones (1839–89), whose parents had emigrated from Brecon to the Pittsburgh area in 1832, just three years before the Carnegie family arrived. Bill Jones grew up in one of the iron-smelting towns of the Pittsburgh area, where his father, the Reverend John Jones, was employed in the industry and was prominent in Welsh religious and cultural circles. It was a home with books: the youngster was well read and (it was later said) could quote Shakespeare as readily as could Andrew Carnegie.[1]

Bill Jones was employed in the iron industry from childhood, and he gained a breadth of experience of various aspects of the industry before enlisting in 1862 on the Union side in the American Civil War. He served until the war's end, rising to the rank of captain; he was proud to continue using his rank during the rest of his life. After the war, Jones joined Andrew Carnegie's steel business, where he was valued in particular as one of the foremost proponents of the Bessemer converter process in North America. He also brought some of his Welsh compatriot workers to the Carnegie works at the same time. Carnegie's tribute to Jones's role at his Edgar Thomson steelworks from 1874 onwards was unstinting: 'So perfect was the machinery, so admirable the plans, so skilful were the men selected by Captain Jones, and so great a manager was he himself, that our success was phenomenal.'[2]

Jones was highly competitive, both personally and professionally – as a young baseball player, and as a steel-maker on whom Carnegie relied heavily as his general superintendent and manager. Jones was steadfastly loyal to Carnegie in return. The only issue of difference between them related to labour costs and fair wages – a difference often resolved on Jones's side of the argument: for Jones, an enlightened business policy was at the same time good business practice. The accident at Carnegie's works that caused Jones's death in 1889 was a heavy personal blow to Carnegie. During the negotiations in 1902–3 for a grant for a new library in Abergavenny, Carnegie recalled that

[Jones] came to me as a working mechanic at 8s. per day. I explained to the captain how several of the younger men in the business department had been made partners and were actually receiving much greater rewards than he, while his services were at least equally valuable, and informed him that we wished to make him a partner. I shall never forget his reply. 'Mr C. I am much obliged, but I know nothing about business and would never wish to be troubled with it – I have plenty to trouble me here in these works. Leave me as I am, and just give me a thundering salary.' Thereafter, I said, the salary of the President of the United States is yours, captain, and so it remained till the sad day of his death. The captain's refusal of partnership was the only one that came within my experience.[3]

Carnegie and his partner Henry C. Frick were honorary pall-bearers at Captain Jones's stately funeral in Pittsburgh in 1889, and Carnegie later erected a monument as a memorial to him in the city.[4]

Carnegie's industrial links with the iron and steel industry in Wales were indirect but were crucial to the future development of his own works. In the late 1870s, following an exploratory visit to Britain by Captain Jones, Carnegie was instrumental in arranging for the American Bessemer Steel Association to purchase the patent of Sidney Gilchrist Thomas's Bessemer converter process for steel-making, which had been invented at Blaenavon and Dowlais in south Wales. In 1881 Thomas visited the Carnegie brothers and their works in New York and Pittsburgh, where he dined with the manager, Captain Bill Jones, whom he thought 'a vigorous and singularly able man'.[5]

Andrew Carnegie was deeply impressed on meeting Sidney Thomas:

The first thought that passed through my mind when I saw him was, 'He's a genius'. I never saw one who so completely separated in himself talent from that indescribable thing we call genius . . . I have never met a man who carried me so completely away as Sidney Thomas did.

Betraying his own prejudices by the way, Carnegie later acknowledged the importance of this invention by Thomas and his young cousin, Percy Gilchrist: 'These two young men . . . did more for Britain's greatness than all the Kings and Queens put together. Moses struck the rock and brought forth water. They struck the useless phosphoric ore and transformed it into steel – a far greater miracle.'[6]

Somewhat later, Carnegie's visits to Scotland brought him in contact with the Liberal politician and prime minister W. E. Gladstone, who was MP for Midlothian from 1880 to 1894, and whose social and political attitudes Carnegie admired. Both in the United States and Great Britain, Carnegie enjoyed the company of the powerful, in industry and politics. After Gladstone's death (in 1898) and the purchase of Skibo castle, he was especially drawn in Britain to politicians in the Liberal party, and it may be no accident that when a number of his libraries in Wales were opened the ceremony was performed by Liberal MPs in David Lloyd George's circle, men like David Davies (at Aberystwyth), D. A. Thomas (at Trecynon and Church Village in Glamorgan), Samuel Thomas Evans (at Skewen) and J. Herbert Lewis (at Rhyl).

Gladstone, moreover, lived at Hawarden in Flintshire, and Carnegie became interested in his plans for an endowed library at Hawarden, which the former prime minister founded in 1894 (stacking the shelves himself!). When the new building of St Deiniol's Library was opened by Earl Spencer in October 1902 as the national memorial to Gladstone, Carnegie attended the ceremony and gave an address. It was not quite the free and public library that Carnegie had in mind for his own grants, but he admired the large religious and cultural collection of 34,000 books which Gladstone had amassed and planned for this unique institution.[7]

Carnegie also formed a close association with David Lloyd George, the Liberal MP for Carnarvon Boroughs from 1890 to 1945. Carnegie could scarcely have failed to be aware of the eisteddfodau which his steelworkers attended in the steel towns of Pennsylvania, and Captain Jones had encouraged him to support the St David's Society and its eisteddfod in Pittsburgh in December 1883. Carnegie himself inherited from his parents a love of music which inspired his numerous grants to purchase organs in churches and chapels in North America and the United Kingdom; like libraries, they could extend the cultural experience of ordinary folk.[8]

It is more than likely that when the Welsh National Eisteddfod was being organized at Bangor in 1902, it was Lloyd George who proposed that Carnegie be invited to be a president at the eisteddfod and arranged that a deputation of 'eminent' Welshmen should wait on him in New York to convey the invitation. As the local newspaper put it ironically, just when a new library was being mooted at Bangor, 'There is, of course, no desire to bleed Mr Carnegie but if there was he is probably able to take care of himself'. In the event Carnegie was unable to attend, but the Bangor library opened in 1907 with a substantial grant of £2,500 from Andrew Carnegie.[9]

Lloyd George was no less prominent in the organization of the National Eisteddfod at Caernarfon in 1906. On this occasion, both the Lord Mayor of London, Sir Walter Vaughan Morgan, whose family hailed from Breconshire, and Andrew Carnegie were invited to be presidents. At nearby Bangor it was hoped that during his visit to north Wales he would open the new public library, receive the freedom of the city and even lay the foundation stone at the University College of North Wales's new buildings. It would indeed have been a red-letter day at Bangor. Carnegie accepted the invitation to the eisteddfod and made a 'munificent donation' to it, but at the last moment he had to withdraw because his only child, Margaret, who was then nine years old, was taken seriously ill.[10]

Carnegie's industrial, political and educational interests are reflected in the part he played in two institutions which brought him in contact with a number of leading patrons of the public library movement in Wales. The Iron and Steel Institute of Great Britain, of which Carnegie was a council member during the 1890s, and indeed its president in 1903–5, awarded him its Bessemer Medal in 1904. At its biannual meetings, which he attended whenever he was in Britain, he could meet prominent industrialists from Wales, especially from Merthyr and Dowlais. At the London meeting in May 1903 he was lobbied by Edward Windsor Richards, a former president of the Institute, on behalf of Rogerstone parish council. Richards, who was born in Dowlais, had worked with Sidney Gilchrist Thomas and had managed the Ebbw Vale works in the past. On 31 March 1903 he advised Rogerstone's council to delay approaching Andrew Carnegie for a grant to build a new library until he had attended the Institute's meeting in May and could pass Rogerstone's appeal for a grant in person to the incoming president – as he evidently did with success within a few weeks.[11] The following year, in May 1904, David Lloyd George attended the Institute's annual meeting and dined with Carnegie: they were doubtless able to chat about Carnegie's support for Cricieth's new library which was in the process of being built, and which Lloyd George and his younger brother William supported.[12]

Carnegie's commitment to the Library Association of Great Britain, founded in 1877 to extend the range and quality of mainly municipal libraries in the United Kingdom, was less direct but just as sympathetic. Among other like-minded champions of public libraries were two significant figures in the Association who were also patrons of Carnegie libraries in Wales. Lord Windsor of St Fagans was president of the Library Association in 1895–6, and towards the end of his term an honorary fellowship of the Association was bestowed on Andrew Carnegie. It was Windsor who in 1899 introduced the bill in the House of Lords to simplify the Public Libraries Act by making more flexible the use of the penny rate and to extend its application to county councils. When, two years later, Carnegie invited applications for grants for the founding of free public libraries, Lord Windsor was one of the first to encourage local authorities in Glamorgan – such as at Trecynon, Merthyr and Penarth – to formulate their plans and submit them to Carnegie.[13]

The Association also acquired an influential advocate in J. Herbert Lewis, lawyer, politician and educationalist, who had been Liberal MP for Flint Boroughs since 1890. Lewis, who became president of the Library Association in 1920–1, had earlier been close to W. E. Gladstone, one of his constituents at Hawarden, and to David Lloyd George, with whom he was on friendly terms. These contacts gave him an entrée to Carnegie's circle too, and Lewis enthusiastically supported both Rhyl and Flint in their successful applications to the millionaire-philanthropist for building grants; later on, as parliamentary secretary at the Board of Education he was also largely responsible for piloting the Public Libraries bill through the House of Commons in 1919, after a long delay.[14]

SIX

CREATING CARNEGIE LIBRARIES

M OST OF THE correspondence – including almost all communications from Wales – between Andrew Carnegie and those who, once they had heard of his passion for founding libraries, bombarded him with hundreds of enquiries and requests every year after 1897 was dealt with by Carnegie's private secretary, James Bertram (1872–1934). It was he who carefully acknowledged receipt of these letters, often seeking further details about local plans before responding with Carnegie's decisions in a succinct and courteous yet somewhat eccentric style – for, like Carnegie himself, Bertram had developed his own form of shorthand and simplified spelling. Carnegie had recruited Bertram in 1897, just when he was negotiating the purchase of Skibo castle in Sutherland. Bertram was born (in 1872) and bred in Corstophine, a village a short distance west of Edinburgh where he attended Daniel Stewart's College. His first job was with the Great Northern and North-Eastern Railway companies in 1888 in Edinburgh itself, and then, to gain further experience, he emigrated to South Africa, where the railway industry was beginning to make rapid strides. He took jobs with the Natal Government Railways and then in the gold mines, and even with the British army. For health reasons, and while still in his twenties, he returned to Scotland in 1897 and applied for the advertised post of private secretary to Andrew Carnegie. Bertram's railway experience may well have appealed to Carnegie, whose involvement with railways in North America had been spectacular from an early stage of his career.

James Bertram spent much time in Carnegie's company, both in the United States of America (especially at the imposing mansion on East 91st Street in New York) and at Skibo castle in Scotland, gradually concentrating on the millionaire's huge library-building programme. He later also became secretary of Andrew Carnegie's main philanthropic vehicle, the Carnegie Corporation of New York, from its inception in 1911. After Carnegie's death in 1919, Bertram continued to serve as secretary of the Corporation as it developed its programmes worldwide. Although Carnegie interested himself from time to time in a number of the individual appeals for funds to create libraries, Bertram came to know his employer's mind sufficiently well to respond to enquiries and requests on his own initiative. He it was who, loyally and conscientiously, implemented the criteria for eligibility for the grants and oversaw the contractual arrangements that were made. As far as is known, Bertram never visited Wales to inspect any of the Carnegie libraries.[1]

He sought expert advice to assist in administering applications and had soon devised a standard 'schedule of questions' to elicit the essential information needed to form a judgement: the name, status and population of the town, whether or not it had a library, and, if it did, where it was housed, whether it was private or public, and how many books it had. The applying authority also had to provide assurances that it owned a freehold site and, crucially, was willing to raise funds through taxation to support a library in the future.[2]

Bertram then decided whether a community had a large enough population to support a library according to Carnegie's principles of grant-giving. He scrutinized the building plans prior to releasing funds in instalments to the organizing committees. By about 1908 he felt the need to try to stabilize the costs of construction because of what he and Carnegie regarded as some of the more extravagant architectural or stylistic embellishments that sometimes seemed to be contemplated at the expense of library space. In 1911 Bertram was the principal author of a pamphlet, *Notes on the Erection of Library Buildings*, which sought to rationalize – though not to standardize in detail – the practical implementation of principles of light and space for the design and layout of the Carnegie-sponsored buildings that had gradually evolved over the past decade and more.[3]

The size of Carnegie's grants was intended to meet the costs of construction, 'complete and ready for use with indispensable furniture and fixtures', and to include the architects' fees.

> Some architects [Bertram commented, occasionally using his own distinctive shorthand] ar liable, unconsciously, no dout, to aim at architectural features and to subordinate useful accommodation. Some ar also apt, on account of a lack of practical knowledge of the administration of a library, to plan interiors which ar entirely unsuited for the purposes of a free public library.

As early as November 1903, he had to relay Carnegie's misgivings about the inclusion of a clock tower in the plans for Colwyn Bay's library, on the grounds that 'it spoils the building' and diverted funds from the library itself.[4]

On the other hand, Carnegie was open to being persuaded to make a supplementary grant available where the construction of a library seemed to warrant it. At Colwyn Bay he may not have liked the proposed clock tower, but he was sufficiently impressed by the town's efforts to match his own £1,500, granted in July 1902, that he doubled his grant in December 1903 – and cleared the building debt of £784 in October 1905![5]

Other considerations weighed with him at Barry, where the construction ran into a problem allegedly because the contractor had departed from his brief, though more likely because of the difficulty encountered in laying satisfactory foundations in what had been part of a former quarry. This led to an acrimonious dispute which lasted a year (1904–5), during which it was even proposed, in September 1904, 'to pull down the building as it now stands and to take up the foundations and to re-lay the foundations and erect the building in accordance with the drawings . . . and the instructions' to the contractor. The dispute between architect and contractor, involving the council and its library committee, eventually required formal arbitration proceedings that cost the building budget an additional £800. Keeping Carnegie informed throughout turned out to be a wise precaution, since in the spring of 1905 he decided to meet the extra cost.[6]

In carefully monitoring the expenditure of funds, Bertram's interventions, sent by telegraph or by sea-post with Carnegie's personal or tacit approval, were not always comfortable for library committees to read, especially when building costs began to spiral, but they were always in the best interest of the libraries themselves. The declared aim was 'To obtain for the money the utmost amount of effective accommodation consistent with good taste in building'. Furthermore, Bertram's pamphlet envisaged the library as a centre for the community that might also promote allied educational and leisure-related activities. Bertram came to request drawings for review and corresponded about designs, though he acknowledged that library committees ultimately had the main influence as the buildings took shape.[7]

As Carnegie's principal private secretary managing the millionaire's philanthropy, the conscientious and serious-minded Bertram bore a heavy burden of paperwork. In March 1904 he wrote with feeling in a postscript to a letter to John Lloyd, the London lawyer and reformer who had been conducting negotiations with Carnegie on behalf of his native town of Brecon. Bertram commented, to some unintended amusement in Brecon when the letter was read to the councillors:

> I wish to draw your attention to the fact we have to carry about with us some thousands of sets of correspondence, and if every correspondent wrote on thick paper and in long-hand, as you do, it would be impossible for us to do business. Your letters weigh between 1lb and 2lb. Will you kindly type-write your communications on thin business paper?[8]

The Carnegie library buildings in Wales, although they were in a variety of styles and sizes, benefited from contemporary developments in the design of library buildings in the United States and the United Kingdom, and from competition among local and national architects for whom the hundreds of new libraries in Great Britain offered a great opportunity.[9] The examples and models available, and James Bertram's consolidated *Notes on the Erection of Library Buildings* of 1911, identified the elements and orientation of the ideal library building that could be applied in even the smaller Welsh libraries. An imposing entrance in a centrally sited frontage was key to the building, as at Newport and Llandudno, creating a welcoming and spacious environment for even the most tentative potential reader. In the larger buildings, such as at Colwyn Bay and Canton in Cardiff, provision was made for a children's room, a large reading room, a reference room, an additional room for use by women (or 'ladies', as the current idiom had it) and a newspaper and magazine space, along with a central hub for librarians who (if available) were encouraged to play a constructive role in planning alongside the architects and contractors.

REE LIBRARY & ROAD. WHITCHURCH.

Figure 2. Whitchurch library, c.1905. One of the earliest photographs of a Carnegie library in Wales, it shows the commanding position which the new library, opened in December 1904, occupied at the heart of the village community (National Library of Wales).

Moreover, increasingly sophisticated designs took into account the peculiar environmental demands of light, air and ventilation that differentiated libraries from most other public buildings – hence the large windows, often a lighted dome, and the careful positioning of tables, seats and stands for newspapers. The advent of electricity could extend significantly opening hours for evening use.

The building programme also encouraged developments in the public architecture of libraries in both America and the United Kingdom. In Wales most of the Carnegie buildings emphasized open access for the public, the separation of reference, lending and reading, and, where possible, children's departments in even the smaller buildings, usually with a central

Figure 3. The bright and welcoming entrance of Cathays library, soon after its opening in March 1907 (from the collections of the National Monuments Record of Wales © Cardiff Libraries).

entrance reception and 'control' desk for the library's staff. For example, at Cathays in Cardiff, where the library was opened in 1907, separate reading rooms were provided for women and for children; while at Treharris the elaborate curved glass-panelled timber reception structure in front of the librarian's desk, dating from 1909, is still in situ.[10] Little was left to chance or undue eccentricity. Where 'the professional experience of architects and the operational experience of librarians' were brought to bear, the most successful libraries resulted.

In Britain the use of red brick or stone, with stone and ceramic dressings, became a common feature of public libraries funded by Carnegie, in contrast to other more dowdy structures. Local library committees were aware of their local responsibilities and, whereas architects might be appointed by open competition that might attract designs from practices across the country, more local interests were often taken into account when engaging building contractors who were, naturally, fewer in number. Thus, at Aberystwyth in the summer of 1904, as many as forty-eight designs were submitted by architects from England and Wales in an open competition, and an external assessor was appointed with the advice of the president of the Society of British Architects. From a shortlist of three, Walter G. Payton of Birmingham was selected and asked to submit his amended designs 'without any avoidable delay'. By contrast, the contract for building the new library was awarded in April 1905 to a local builder, Messrs Edwards Bros of Trefechan, taking the advice of Walter G. Payton as the chosen architect, even though the contractors submitting the nine tenders ranged from Birmingham, Shrewsbury and Oswestry to Aberystwyth itself.[11]

Advocacy within the library committees in favour of local employment doubtless took place, as it did at Abergavenny. After the Carnegie grant was offered to the town in 1902, a local architect, B. J. Francis, offered books for the new library provided his designs were accepted. However, the library committee decided on an open competition, prompting a petition from the Amalgamated Society of Carpenters and Joiners of Abergavenny on 2 November 1904 to reconsider the confidentiality of the tender. The society urged that a local firm should be favoured 'as the state of trade in Abergavenny is not everything that could be desired' and there was no prospect of improvement in the near future. This would provide employment to local men. In the event, only two submissions were made; the sealed bid chosen was in fact Francis's. The building contract was then awarded to Henry Smith of Wolverley, near Kidderminster, some distance away.[12]

SEVEN

BUILDING THE CARNEGIE LIBRARIES OF WALES

I N WALES, as in the United Kingdom generally, the Carnegie libraries were created especially in the industrial towns and villages and commercial centres where the populations were considered large enough to support them – places like Brynmawr, Pontypool and Rogerstone in the south Wales valleys, ports like Newport and Cardiff, the slate-quarrying centres of Deiniolen and Bangor, northern coalfield towns like Coedpoeth (or Bersham) and Wrexham, market towns like Aberystwyth and Abergavenny, and even in spas and tourist centres such as Llandudno and Llandrindod Wells. In contrast to the miners' libraries, Carnegie foundations were established in semi-rural as well as in urban and small industrial locations in various parts of Wales. In some of these places the new library buildings were the first secular public buildings to be built alongside the nineteenth-century churches and nonconformist chapels.[1]

Immediately after the announcement of Carnegie's philanthropic intentions in 1901, there was no common prospectus available inviting formal and detailed applications; rather, the approaches and letters came from individuals, authorities and organizations over the next decade and more as a result of the publicity that his burgeoning philanthropy attracted. For example, interest at Tai-bach, near Margam, was kindled in 1902 by the news that Bridgend, not far away, had recently made a successful application for funding.[2]

Figure 4. 'HER TURN NEXT. Dame Cardiff: "I wonder if he will think of us!"' J. M. Staniforth's cartoon (*Western Mail*, 4 July 1902) depicts smiling ladies, representing Merthyr Tydfil, Bridgend and Barry, receiving some of 'Carnegie's Millions', while a hopeful Cardiff hovers in the vicinity.

It may not be fortuitous that the first approach from a Welsh community, in September 1901, came from Buckley in Flintshire, which was but a couple of miles from Hawarden, where the Gladstone library had recently been established – and whose opening was attended by Carnegie himself. It may be that the local council at Buckley had advance news of Carnegie's intentions earlier in the year, and certainly Herbert Gladstone offered £100 to assist in creating a new library. Indeed, an enterprising young businessman and local Liberal politician from Wrexham, Edward Hughes, wrote to Carnegie as early as the beginning of March 1901, enclosing a copy of a book about John Wilkinson (1728–1808), the ironmaster who had developed the furnaces at nearby Bersham, convinced that Carnegie would find it interesting.[3] Hughes may or may not have been aware that Carnegie already had an interest in Wilkinson's ironworks at Bersham through his studies of James Watt, the Scottish inventor and engineer, and his long-time partner, Matthew Boulton, the Birmingham manufacturer. Watt and Boulton drew on the expertise of Wilkinson and his steam engine, and a century later they figured prominently in Andrew Carnegie's biography of James Watt, which was published in 1905.[4] Whether or not Edward Hughes was attempting to plant a seed in Carnegie's mind on behalf of Wrexham and its area, the town itself did not pursue the possibility of a Carnegie library until a year later, in 1902.

The second approach from Wales arrived from Cricieth a month later. it may have been no accident that the home of David Lloyd George, whom Carnegie had come to know well, was no more than two miles from the town.[5] Thereafter the news of Carnegie's philanthropy spread rapidly. In October 1901 the commercial centres of Barry, Penarth and Bridgend, all in Glamorgan, were in touch with Carnegie's office, and in 1902–3 more than twenty others followed suit. At Brynmawr, near the northern rim of the coalfield in what was then Breconshire, a special meeting of the urban district council was held on 9 July 1902 when it was resolved to approach Andrew Carnegie,'the famous philanthropist for help to establish a Public Library and Reading Room' in the town.[6]

SITES

The Public Libraries Acts provided a framework which could be adapted to suit Carnegie's philosophy of supporting the cultural aspirations and ambitions of all classes in society. He aimed to provide funds with which to build permanent, purpose-built public libraries where communities were prepared to help themselves to achieve their ambitions and where wealthy landowners and industrialists, even religious bodies and local authorities, might be persuaded to emulate his own philanthropy, albeit on a modest scale, by offering appropriate sites free of charge. His substantial gifts thus encouraged local benefactors to make the sites available. They also relieved the burden on the penny rate so that more could be spent on the purchase of books and newspapers so as to grow the library and to engage professional librarians, and perhaps also to increase the flow of donations of books and collections from individual patrons. Appeals for donations of books of the broadest of taste might be sent worldwide, as in the case of Abergavenny.

The most fundamental of the qualifications for a Carnegie library grant was the applicant's provision of a freehold site for the building which would be funded by the grant (including the architect's fees) and therefore would not be a burden on the rates or prejudice the library's future management.

Carnegie was well aware that especially the smaller authorities might not have a freehold site readily available, but he hoped that his own example would be followed by others more locally; indeed, in some quarters it was ruefully regretted that local landowners and industrialists did not readily emulate the philanthropy of Andrew Carnegie. It is true that some authorities took steps to acquire suitable sites themselves. The town council of Flint was modest in its proposals (and therefore in its appeal to Carnegie through the local MP, J. Herbert Lewis). In August 1902 Carnegie informed Lewis that he would give £200 to the council to refashion as a library the market hall underneath the large town hall assembly room. About the same time, and not far away, the industrial and market town of Holywell was unsuccessful in its bid for a Carnegie grant, despite having J. Herbert Lewis's support. The reason given in a letter from James Bertram was that the town council was not prepared to erect a new building but proposed adapting its existing library and using any grant for other purposes.[7]

Rhyl's town council was more ambitious, and offered the site of an old bank and the old police station which would extend the existing town hall to create a purpose-built library; ambitious, too, was its request for substantial funding. Carnegie was initially prepared to offer £3,000 in 1903 on the understanding that the proposed library would be a separate building provided by the council. In the event, the plan to build an extension to the town hall and devote only £2,000 to the library and the remaining £1,000 to the town hall itself did not go down well with Carnegie when he heard about it in the winter of 1904–5. His reaction caused 'consternation' in the town and, while he approved the plans for the new building beside the town hall, his reassertion that the £3,000 should be spent on the library itself was evidently accepted. The foundation stone of the new Carnegie library was laid in January 1906.[8]

In Wrexham, which already had a small public library in the town hall, the corporation acquired several properties in 1898, including the Yspyty property which it offered as the site for a new Carnegie library, though not until 1904 did the council finally light upon the Guildhall site in what became Queen's Square.[9]

In south Wales, the branch library at Abercanaid was provided by Merthyr urban district council when it bought a leased site from the owners of the Wingfield and Mackintosh estate for a little over £100. Matters were less straightforward at Aberystwyth. Although the town owned the site in Alfred Place, on Corporation Street, that was proposed for the new library, it was leased by a local clergyman who was reluctant

to surrender his lease without substantial recompense; lengthy negotiations took place before the issue was resolved and the Carnegie building
could be started.[10]

However, not all authorities were able to provide a site, and private,
local philanthropy was sought, probably in the majority of cases. This came
from a variety of sources, sometimes at the urging of councils. At Colwyn
Bay, a wealthy tourist centre, a public subscription appeal was launched
to acquire a site and thereby secure Carnegie's grant of £3,800 to build a
large and impressive building. To qualify for the very first Carnegie grant
in Wales, for a new library at Buckley in Flintshire, W. E. Gladstone's son,
Herbert Gladstone, and the vicar of Buckley and his wife together offered
£700 to purchase the freehold of a site near Buckley's church which was
on the road towards Hawarden, the Gladstone home. But another offer, of
a site in a central position in Buckley adjoining the council offices, came
from two Chester businessmen, Robert and Thomas Griffiths, and for a
short while 'a battle of the sites' ensued. The latter offer was eventually
accepted and Andrew Carnegie's grant of £1,600 secured.[11]

A more awkward issue arose at Llandudno, where there had been a
town library since 1873 on a site leased from Lord Mostyn. Moreover, this
site was encumbered by a mortgage and in 1907 discussions were still
taking place with the current Lord Mostyn to secure its freehold; in any
case, it was only recently that the Public Libraries Act had been adopted
by Llandudno council.[12] At first, Andrew Carnegie declined to authorize
payment of the £4,000 that he had made available as early as 1903 for
Llandudno's new library on the same site, but eventually Lord Mostyn was
prevailed upon to gift the freehold to the council outright.[13]

At Cricieth, the Cambrian Railway Co. offered a choice of sites on its
own property, but the urban district council declined both and instead
chose a site near the railway station that was offered by J. T. Jones of Parciau, the chairman of Cricieth's council.[14]

By contrast, in industrial south Wales there was a greater reliance on the
generosity of landowners-turned-industrialists. Emily Talbot (died 1918),
the heiress of the vast Talbot estate of Margam abbey and Penrice castle in
Gower, was a generous patron of cultural and religious causes in Glamorgan, and in 1911 she responded to an appeal from Margam urban district
council with the promise of a site in the industrial suburb of Tai-bach. The
campaign for a new library in the Aberavon area had begun in 1902, though
it encountered a certain amount of local opposition and it was not until
1904 that the council was able to adopt the Public Libraries Act, which was

a prerequisite if Carnegie were also to be approached. Only in 1911 was progress made, and then the canny Miss Talbot insisted on a special covenant to her gift of a site, whereby any building on it should never be used for any other purpose than for a library for public use in perpetuity. Andrew Carnegie responded with a grant of £2,000 which he increased to £2,500 by the time the foundation stone was laid for Tai-bach's library in 1914.[15]

Winifred Coombe Tennant, who lived near Neath, moved in similar circles though she was a much younger woman (1874–1956). She too was an enthusiastic supporter of culture and the arts in south Wales and a vigorous campaigner for women's suffrage before the First World War. Later a Liberal politician and supporter of Lloyd George, in the Edwardian decade she sponsored the library movement in the Neath area and as a tenant-for-life of the Tennant estate she persuaded the trustees in 1904 to donate a site in Skewen, near Neath, for a 'free library and reading room'. It was a complicated legal transaction, but in June 1905 the conveyance was agreed. Andrew Carnegie in his turn donated £2,000.[16]

In Bridgend and Rogerstone the respective lords lieutenant of Glamorgan and Monmouthshire were prevailed upon to make freehold sites available. In March 1905, the earl of Dunraven, of Dunraven castle near the Vale's coast, a Conservative politician and himself a writer, agreed to defray three-quarters of the cost of a site in the middle of Bridgend, with the town raising the rest (£150) by subscription. Andrew Carnegie offered £2,000 to erect the building.[17]

A year earlier, Lord Tredegar, politician and soldier and a benefactor of several Newport causes, had needed little persuasion to promise a prime site at Rogerstone overlooking the broad Ebbw valley north-west of Newport. The parish council had adopted the Public Libraries Act some ten years earlier and in approaching Andrew Carnegie it had a valuable ally locally in the deputy-lieutenant of Monmouthshire, Edward Windsor Richards. Richards, born in Dowlais, was an engineer and steel-maker who had worked with Sidney Gilchrist Thomas; moreover, he was a former president of the Iron and Steel Institute, whose current president was none other than Andrew Carnegie. Richards advised the council on 31 March 1903 to delay approaching Carnegie until after the May meeting of the Institute, presumably so that he could press Rogerstone's case. His advocacy evidently succeeded because James Bertram had replied by 25 August with Carnegie's promise of a grant of £1,400, provided the site was held in freehold. Lord Tredegar duly obliged, and when the building was opened by him in November 1905 he also offered some books to the new library.[18]

No less helpful was the duke of Beaufort, deputy-lieutenant of Breconshire and with an even greater landowning presence in south-east Wales. After Andrew Carnegie offered the sum of £1,250 for a new library at Brynmawr in 1903, the duke provided a virgin site in the iron-mining town, together with a large collection of books. In July 1907 the duke and duchess of Beaufort travelled to Brynmawr to inspect the library and the adjacent institute which together were described by an enthusiastic reporter as being 'worthy of the city of the hills'.[19]

John Capel Hanbury (1853–1921) of Pontypool Park, whose family's fortunes were built on the tinplate industry in the eighteenth century, eventually offered 'an admirable site nearby opposite the town hall' and the police station in Pontypool's main street. But the campaign proceeded less smoothly than elsewhere. In May 1903 the urban district council resolved, along with the local literary institute, to approach Andrew Carnegie for a large grant of £8,000. Ever concerned to assemble all the facts, in January 1904 James Bertram, acting on Carnegie's behalf, asked for a 'picture' of the existing library, and not until the following November was Bertram able to write from New York offering a more modest £2,800 to the council, provided it adopted the Public Libraries Act and was able to raise the rateable sum of £85 per annum mentioned in its original letter, together with a supplement of £25 per annum to guarantee satisfactory maintenance of any new building. That still left the question of a freehold site, which was unresolved until 10 January 1906 when Hanbury and his fellow lords of the manor of Wentsland formally agreed to gift the site opposite the town hall to the council for the new library.[20] Nevertheless it was another year before, on 4 December 1906, Carnegie authorized payment up to a revised sum of £2,000 so that building work could begin. Delays had been caused by the late adoption of the Public Libraries Act, as from 31 August, by Carnegie's unease about amendments to the plan to include a caretaker's premises in the basement instead of a public lecture room, and by Hanbury's minor reservations about the placing of some windows (which might perhaps have overlooked his mansion).[21]

In contrast, Lord Windsor of St Fagans had already been a generous supporter of cultural causes in Penarth when, in September 1903, he was glad to be able to offer a site for a library in the town that was both centrally situated and easily accessible from all parts of Penarth. He was a past president of the Library Association of Great Britain and supported the public library movement in several communities in Glamorgan.[22]

Figure 5. Penarth library, *c.*1905. This early photograph shows the library's prime site on the corner of Stanwell Road and Rectory Road, donated by Lord Windsor; the library was opened in 1905 (National Library of Wales).

It may well have been a personal disappointment to Andrew Carnegie that the plans for several libraries in the pre-eminent industrial centre of Merthyr Tydfil proceeded even less smoothly than at Pontypool. After some hesitation, the Public Libraries Act was adopted by Merthyr urban district council in 1899 and an ambitious scheme for a new central library and six branch libraries was placed before Andrew Carnegie in 1902. He responded with the offer of a substantial grant of £6,000, which was increased in subsequent years to more than £12,000, provided freehold sites were secured by the council and the whole revenue of the rate assessment were devoted to buying books and to the general upkeep of the buildings. In 1905 his total donation reached £12,500 specifically to mark the granting of borough status to Merthyr. Carnegie went out of his way to instruct his secretary, James Bertram, to explain to D. A. Thomas, the local Liberal MP who had forwarded the original plans to him, that 'Mr C. is induced to do this because of his indebtedness to the Welsh element in America, many of whom have rendered him service. Mr C. says "they are a great people, the Welsh". He brackets them with the Scotch.' Yet it proved to be a major undertaking to secure freehold sites at all seven sites, at Treharris, Aberfan, Troedyrhiw, Abercanaid, Penydarren (each initially granted £700 by Carnegie) and Dowlais (granted £1,000), as well as for a central library at Merthyr itself (initially granted £1,500).[23]

Several of the branch libraries materialized in short order, well before the central library could be built. At Troedyrhiw, a freehold site was given by Lord Windsor, while a leasehold site was available at Penydarren at a nominal rent. Less favourable was the situation a short distance away at Abercanaid, where a leasehold site had to be purchased from the local Wingfield and Mackintosh estate for a little over £100 in order to establish a branch library and reading room by the end of 1902. At the opening of the latter library in the following January, praise was heaped on Andrew Carnegie for his financial support while (it was reported ruefully) 'the local magnates which had made large fortunes in connection with the industries of the place' had given nothing and had even opposed the library movement.[24] Such comments in the press may have prompted a conspicuous exception in Guest, Keen and Nettlefolds, the iron and steel conglomerate whose origins lay in the Dowlais Iron Company, where Thomas and Gilchrist had developed the Bessemer process half a century earlier. GKN sponsored the largest of Merthyr's branch libraries by gifting the elevated site above Dowlais and its world-famous works, where the new library opened in January 1907. A modern plaque on the library records GKN's gift.

The sixth and last of the branches to be opened was at Treharris, in 1909, with space for 3,600 books. There had been a temporary hitch the previous year when James Bertram, acting on behalf of Andrew Carnegie, declined to authorize additional funding on the grounds that Carnegie did not wish the building to be used for other than library purposes (as presumably was proposed).[25]

Ironically, and despite the progress with Merthyr's branch libraries, a new central library was much delayed. The council's plan to acquire the large Shiloh Welsh Wesleyan Chapel in Merthyr for £3,000 fell through at an early stage.[26] And then the First World War supervened. At the time

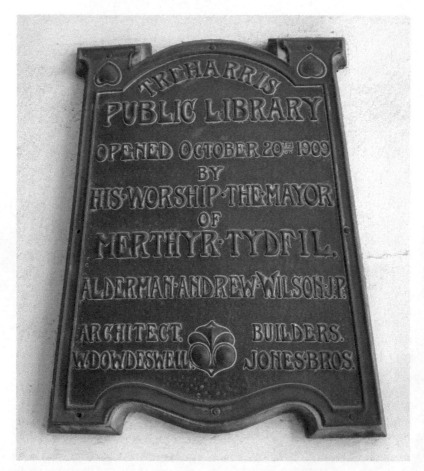

Figure 6. The plaque marking the opening of Treharris's library in October 1909 by the mayor of Merthyr Tydfil, Alderman Andrew Wilson JP. It notes both the architect, William Dowdeswell, and the builder, Jones Bros.

of Andrew Carnegie's death in 1919 the central library still had not been built and the era of Edwardian beneficence had come to an end. However, the Carnegie UK Trust kept faith with Merthyr and eventually, in 1935, the new library was opened at the heart of the borough.[27]

Both Carnegie and local library committees recognized that even with the income from the penny rate, libraries would be hard pressed to maintain a flow of books and newspapers for their readers and borrowers and to sustain the fabric of the new libraries and their modest staff. Additional income was welcomed, from a variety of often imaginative sources. Implementing this prospectus proved too great a challenge for some district and parish councils that aspired to a Carnegie grant. It is perhaps surprising that the borough of Cowbridge, a marketing centre in the Vale of Glamorgan with Roman and medieval antecedents, encountered insurmountable difficulty in meeting the Carnegie criteria. The borough council contemplated appealing to Andrew Carnegie in November 1903 but quickly realized that, unlike other councils nearby, it could not meet the criteria – or else James Bertram dashed their hopes of doing so – for they did not pursue the matter. Cowbridge had asked for a grant for their existing reading room and library in order to purchase books and meet 'general management purposes'. The intention was likely to appeal to Carnegie – 'so as to place the Rooms within the reach of the Artisan Classes, for whose benefit, primarily, they were provided'. But other of the council's proposals ran counter to his philanthropic principles: it had no plans to adopt the Public Libraries Act because the population was small and a 3s. 4d rate would produce only £12 10s. 0d a year; moreover, it proposed to levy a subscription of 6s. per annum for use of the library, and there was no other endowment available. Cowbridge did not, therefore, acquire a Carnegie library.[28]

A similar situation occurred at Haverfordwest in Pembrokeshire, even though it was a much larger market town, also of medieval foundation. It had, too, grander ambitions and, initially, strong support among the Liberal establishment for a new library in the town. The first approach to Andrew Carnegie was made in August 1902, but when a reply arrived belatedly in June 1903 seeking more information about the town's plans, there was no local consensus of opinion and some resentment at Carnegie's reply. More serious obstacles appeared by 1906 when the idea of a library was canvassed anew. In the meantime, Henry Owen of Poston, Pembrokeshire, a noted historian and antiquary, especially of Pembrokeshire, offered to bequeath his large collection of books and manuscripts to the county, and this was linked to a suggestion that Haverfordwest's castle should be adapted to house them in a new library launched by subscription. The Liberal MP for Pembrokeshire, John Wynford Philipps (1898–1908), had taken an initiative and prepared a plan, while his younger brother, Owen Philipps, who became MP for Pembroke and Haverfordwest in 1906, gave his support, and this combination was doubtless responsible for persuading Gladstone's biographer, John Morley, who happened to be the secretary of state for India in Campbell-Bannerman's Liberal cabinet, to put the request for a grant to his friend, Andrew Carnegie. It was the Liberal caucus at work. Both Morley and Owen Philipps had strong Scottish connections and are likely to have known Carnegie well: it was Carnegie who had presented to Morley the late Lord Acton's extensive library in July 1902, while Philipps had been a successful shipping businessman in Glasgow before he entered politics. However, Haverfordwest's proposals departed in several respects from the principles to which Carnegie adhered in making his grants – especially on the matter of a site and the resort to subscription – and they were not pursued.[29]

ARCHITECTS AND BUILDERS

The libraries sponsored by Carnegie in Edwardian Wales were designed by local architects in some cases and in others after inviting plans more widely, and they were generally built by local contractors in a variety of styles, both historic and contemporary – Classical, neo-Gothic, Renaissance, Baroque, art deco, Arts and Crafts, and a few that defy classification. Almost all seem to have been conversant with the prevailing architectural styles used in public buildings at the turn of the twentieth century, and indeed helped to popularize them. Most of the libraries still stand and a number of them enjoy the state's protection as listed buildings.[30]

Town and parish councils, and their library committees, were keen to commission libraries that would be notable buildings for a notable purpose in their own communities, within the financial constraints imposed by Andrew Carnegie's grants and any independent funds that they had available. They were conscious too that designs and plans would be scrutinized by Carnegie and his private secretary. Hence, as at Aberystwyth, there was an open competition at Wrexham, where as many as 104 architects submitted plans. They were judged by the senior Liverpool architect and designer of the Cunard building in the city, W. E. Willink; Vernon Hodge, of Teddington, London, was selected to design Wrexham's new library.[31]

Even the somewhat smaller library proposed for Pontypool elicited nineteen architects' plans within a budget of £1,800 as dictated by Carnegie's grant. These were submitted to Mr Swash of the well-established Newport practice of Swash and Bain (which had just completed the Carnegie library at Rogerstone) as 'a professional assessor' in December 1905. The youthful and innovative practice of Speir and Beavan of Cardiff, which had been engaged for Cathays library the previous year, was appointed Pontypool's architects on 26 January 1906. As many as fifteen tenders for the building work were received from contractors across south Wales and the West Country; local considerations doubtless led to the choice of W. N. Campbell of Pontypool.[32]

Another open competition was arranged for the branch library at Treharris. The winner was William Dowdeswell, a local architect, though the contractor was Frank Ekers of Newport.[33] Some sort of competition was also organized at Barry, where thirty-two plans were submitted to an assessor nominated by the president of the British Society of Architects in November 1902, and at the penultimate stage three were placed on public view. The prizewinning design was that of Charles E. Hutchinson and E. Harding Payne of London; of the ten tenders for carrying out the work, the lowest was accepted, submitted by Watkin Williams of Cardiff, doubtless because he had already been engaged for the new post office and government buildings in Barry.[34]

The two large branch libraries in Cardiff, at Cathays and Canton, were made grants by Carnegie of £5,000 apiece in 1903. It took a while to settle on the two sites made available by the town council and to raise a supportive fund of £1,000. Eventually, in February 1905 it was resolved to invite plans for the two libraries from architects 'who have been in practice as principals in Cardiff for not less than six months', judging that there was a corps of architects available in Wales's largest town – soon to be a city. At the same time, an architect of national reputation should be appointed as the council's professional assessor. Within a few months twenty designs had been submitted to the assessor, Henry Vaughan Lanchester of London, who had recently been the architect of Cardiff's stately City Hall and Law Courts in Cathays Park. His first choices were adopted: the highly experienced and veteran architect E. M. Bruce Vaughan of Cardiff and his practice for Canton's library and the younger practice of Speir and Beavan for the more spacious site in Cathays. They were both leading practices in Cardiff, with Vaughan nearing the end of a long career of building churches and domestic and public buildings right across south Wales. At Cathays, Speir and Beavan produced a more striking and innovative 'butterfly' design in Arts and Crafts style.[35] Lanchester's second choices might have raised some eyebrows at their coincidence: he ranked Speir and Beavan runners-up for Canton, and Bruce Vaughan for Cathays![36]

No less predictable, perhaps, though for a different reason, was the appointment of G. A. Humphreys at Llandudno. An architect by training, he was the surveyor and agent of the Mostyn estate, which had gifted the site for the library that was duly opened by Lord Mostyn himself. A local contractor, Edward Owen, executed the designs. But there was some irritation in the town caused by the negotiations with Lord Mostyn over the freehold of the site, and in May 1906 the architects of the area protested that there had not been an open competition, especially when Humphreys was also secretary of the existing library committee. Humphreys was well qualified enough, but it all had the air of a conflict of several interests.[37]

By contrast, no qualms seem to have been voiced at Colwyn Bay about the appointment of John Porter (of Porter and Hunter), who had been born in Colwyn Bay and trained at the Manchester firm of architects that was centrally involved in the development of the seaside resort in the last decades of the nineteenth century.[38] Other councils relied on their local authority architects. The Caernarfonshire county architect worked with a local contractor at Cricieth, while at Newport the new branch library was built by J. H. Williams from designs prepared by the borough architect on the corporation's own freehold land. At Tai-bach John Cox, the district surveyor of Margam urban district council, planned both the new library 'most artistically designed' in Classical style and a public building on the opposite side of the main road.[39]

Several of the towns of north Wales cast the net widely for their designs, whereas the more densely populated industrial centres of the south had a wider range of regional architects nearer to hand. At Bangor, to take another example, the council took its cue from Aberystwyth in organizing a competition, as a result of which the Manchester practice of A. E. Dixon and C. H. Potter was engaged as the architect while Messrs Hughes and Stirling, of Bootle (Liverpool) and London, were the builders. By contrast, at Church Village (or Llantwit Fardre) in Glamorgan, Arthur Llewelyn Thomas of nearby Pontypridd was the architect and Messrs Price Bros of Cardiff the contractors for an unusually distinctive building 'in a free treatment of the Renaissance style'.[40]

ARCHITECTURAL STYLES

Carnegie libraries frequently stand out as landmark buildings for the stone used in their construction and the architectural designs of their architects, as well as for their prominent siting at the heart of communities. They adapted the rich variety of styles available to British architects in the late Victorian and Edwardian eras, many of which were represented in Wales, while being constrained by costs and sometimes, it must be said, by the views of local committees and of Andrew Carnegie and his private secretary.

The two-storey library at Aberystwyth was built of local stone in an Edwardian neo-Classical style of the seventeenth century, with decorative red sandstone bandings and dressings and a slate roof. It stands out, too, because of the art nouveau lettering over the panelled doorway and the green glazed tiles and foliage decoration which adorned the interior.[41] Dowlais's library, of Pennant stone, also with red sandstone dressings and a slate roof, is in a freer Arts and Crafts style of the seventeenth century, but likewise with art nouveau carved details, including 'Public Library' highlighted over the entrance and (though much eroded) carved cartouches on each side.[42]

Art nouveau craftsmanship is widespread in these Welsh libraries, especially in glass; it gives an imposing decorative distinction and warmth to the libraries, such as those at Treharris and Church Village in Glamorgan. No less elaborate are the Edwardian neo-Baroque libraries at Wrexham, Bangor, Llandudno and Barry. At Wrexham, the ground floor is of stone whereas the upper storey is of red brick, with a small square cupola flooding light from above. The curved pediment above the central window has a cartouche in it. Similar in some of its details is Bangor's library: a single-storey building of red brick with ashlar dressings, a central dome with art nouveau decoration inside and an octagonal porch. Above the entrance is the lettering 'Llyfrgell Rhydd [Free Library] 1907', which is appropriate for a largely Welsh-speaking town.[43]

Barry's library, standing to the right of a clock tower, is of two storeys in red brick with Bath stone dressings and tall Ionic columns. The Venetian window on the first floor is surmounted by a cartouche in full relief with flanking female figures said to personify Justice.[44] Quite different from these is Abergavenny's library. This was built in a neo-Gothic style in keeping with Holy Trinity Church opposite in Baker Street and dating from half a century earlier. The stone walls have contrasting ashlar dressings, and high on the front gable is a sculpted figure of Minerva holding a book, with on each side of the entrance porch two sculpted heads of the marquess of Abergavenny (who opened the library) and Andrew Carnegie (who largely financed it).[45]

At the other extreme are several small libraries that were constructed in a more domestic or cottage style. The compact building at Cricieth is of two storeys, the ground floor of red Ruabon brick with stone dressings, the upper part roughcast with ornamental red bricks; the inner entrance door has stained glass, again in art nouveau style.[46] Less richly elaborate were the three branch libraries built a few miles apart in the upper Taff valley, at Aberfan, Abercanaid (where it has since been demolished) and Troedyrhiw, though each had tall windows of neo-Gothic style .

This impressive and imaginative – even occasionally eccentric – range of styles, even in modest-sized buildings, reflects the architectural proclivities of contemporary designers and architects, the abilities of building contractors to implement their designs, and the ideas of local committees, which conscientiously took the final decisions on behalf of the public, yet within the guidelines provided by Andrew Carnegie and James Bertram to ensure that the most up-to-date library facilities were placed within the buildings themselves. Perhaps among the more unusual or 'free' structures are those at Cathays, with its Arts and Crafts suggestions, and Church Village (or Llantwit Fardre) with its Renaissance overtones.

Although Carnegie did not insist that his name should appear on the façade of the libraries which he sponsored, whether in the United Kingdom or in North America, local authorities and library committees in Wales were eager to commemorate his benefactions, especially at the laying of foundation stones and when the buildings were formally opened. Carnegie was much keener to express, whenever possible, his own philosophy and he duly recommended to committees 'that there should be placed over the entrance to the Libraries I build a representation of the rays of a rising sun, and above "Let there be light"'.[47]

However, a local sense of gratitude often outran his modesty. Perhaps as many as a third of Carnegie libraries in Wales trumpeted their principal benefactor on the main façade or over the doorway: thus, the 'Carnegie Free Library' at Tai-bach and Skewen, the 'Carnegie Public Library' at Abergavenny and Brynmawr, the 'Carnegie Library' at Merthyr Tydfil, and, most elaborate of all in reflecting his philosophy, the 'Carnegie Library Free to the Public' at both Cathays and Canton in Cardiff. At Abergavenny the architect went further, adding the portraits in stone of Carnegie and the marquess of Abergavenny. It may be that the small bust of a bearded man which appears beside the doorway at Church Village should also be taken to represent Andrew Carnegie.

As to an appropriate maxim to inspire library users, his own recommendation seems not to have been followed in Wales, but similar maxims were occasionally adopted: at both Church Village and Penarth, in

Figure 7. A sculpted portrait of Andrew Carnegie on a corbel at the entrance to Abergavenny's library, which was opened in September 1906 by the marquess of Abergavenny, whose own image appears on the other side of the entrance.

Welsh, 'Goreu Arf Arf Dysg' (The Best Weapon is the Weapon of Learning) greeted the public. Another adage, in Welsh but now partly eroded, may be seen above the entrance to Treharris's library.

Local authorities and their architects had a certain latitude – within the available funds – to decide on the architectural details of their Carnegie buildings, and in some cases were imaginative in proclaiming the special purpose of the libraries and arousing the interest of their users. The figure of Minerva, the Roman goddess of learning, is regularly associated with educational and library buildings in North America and the United Kingdom, sometimes with military connotations. In Treharris the façade has a shield with a female figure, surely Minerva, with a spear and two swords as if campaigning for the spread of learning, alongside 'Free Library'.[48] At Abergavenny the sculpted representation of Minerva holds a book aloft, while at Barry a cartouche with female figures is more likely to personify education and learning than (as has been suggested) justice.[49]

Although Andrew Carnegie was often invited by grateful communities to the opening of their libraries and/or to the laying of their foundation stones, he was rarely able to accept the invitations – and never, it seems, in Wales. He may too have felt it unwise to single out one or two among the very many of the libraries he sponsored, but in responding to an invitation he might convey 'his best wishes for [the library's] success and the happiness of all the people' as he did of Aberystwyth and Newport.[50] Rather, these ceremonies were attended by local elites whose patronage was thereby engaged and acknowledged. At Abergavenny, it was the marquess of Abergavenny who opened the new library building in 1906, but in the following year Carnegie himself arrived in the town, both to inspect the new library and to receive the freedom of the town in a lavish civic ceremony. Indeed, he eventually achieved a tally of fifty-seven freedoms around the country, usually in towns where he had supported the public library movement, and in ceremonies which he evidently enjoyed.[51]

INSIDE THE LIBRARIES

James Bertram's exchange of letters with library committees reflects the ideas of contemporary planners in America and Britain about the functions and design of public libraries, to which Carnegie's philosophy of philanthropy contributed. At Aberystwyth, S. B. Russell, the respected architect from Hertfordshire whom the president of the Society of British Architects had recommended as an assessor for the appointment of an architect, commented on the constricted nature of the site on Corporation Street and the importance that needed to be attached to the layout of the rooms and the provision of sufficient light for those who used them. The comments were taken on board by Walter G. Payton, the architect, and reported to Carnegie's office.[52]

Of course, the extent to which the desirable elements of a library could be incorporated in the plans depended on the size of the buildings, especially in Wales where a number of them were quite small: at one extreme stood the libraries at Deiniolen and Troedyrhiw; at the other were those at Cathays and Colwyn Bay. Spaces for reading, reference and lending were fundamental to them all. The eagle-eyed Bertram sometimes raised a query or two. In July 1904 he wrote to the secretary of Abergavenny's library committee acknowledging receipt of the plans but drawing attention to what seemed to be a mistake: Carnegie had offered money for a library building, but the current plan showed only two rooms for the library and three for a technical school and a bedroom to boot. Bertram sought an explanation.[53] In the event, Abergavenny's library, which was built during 1905, consisted of a large entrance hall with provision for bicycles, a reading room to the right, a lending library to the left, and provision for 6,500 volumes. A museum was situated on the floor above.[54]

The larger building at Wrexham had separate rooms for the library's several departments. On the ground floor was a general reading room to seat fifty, a ladies' room for about twenty, a reference room and a lending library to accommodate c.20,000 volumes. On the first floor was a large lecture hall that could seat 200. Even the modest library at Cricieth could boast a 'ladies' waiting room' and a 'gentlemen's retiring room', as well as a lofty, light and airy reading room with bookcases for 6,000 books (and space for 3,000 more if needed), a lending library and, on the first floor, a reference room and a committee room.[55]

The largest libraries in Wales provided separate facilities for children. At Penarth the 'boys' reading room' was located in the basement, while at both Canton and Cathays in Cardiff there was a 'children's reading hall'.

The latter are intended [it was noted in 1907] to meet the wants of those children who have no place at home where they can sit and read, who are encouraged to go out into the streets to wander about till bedtime, in order that they may be out of the way, and in small cramped rooms the temptation is great to adopt this rough and ready method of saving trouble and avoiding the necessity of home discipline. These children are consequently apt to pick up bad habits and to suffer in health from exposure to all sorts of weather. It is hoped that these Halls will attract them and help them to better things.

The library committee that managed both Canton and Cathays libraries reported further and appreciatively in 1907 that the open-access arrangements at Canton were working well:

There have been neither losses nor inconveniences, while the educational value to the readers has been considerable . . . At first they were bewildered by the number of books available. Their knowledge of authors was confined to those whose names are prominent

Figures 8a, 8b. Two photographs of the rooms at Cathays library available to boys and girls, smartly dressed for the occasion, and supervised by two of the librarians, one female and the other male. The photographs date from soon after the library's opening in March 1907 (from the collections of the National Monuments Record of Wales © Cardiff Libraries).

in the current periodicals and newspapers. They knew next to nothing of the great writers of the past in any branch of literature. In the course of a few months, however, a great change occurred, and the works of the great masters of English literature are now being steadily read by people who owe their first acquaintance with their authors to the opportunities of examining the books on the shelves of the Canton Library.[56]

The attractions of the library sometimes needed reinforcing with an element of discipline. A few years after the library at Abergavenny was opened, a poster sought to correct the behaviour of some of the 'lads' in the library by warning them that they 'will be taken at once before the Bench of Magistrates, and that punishment by Act of Parliament is "Whipping"!'[57]

Careful thought went into the choice of fittings and furniture. At Aberystwyth it was decided that the furnishings should be in American oak, at a cost of £1,285, while members of the library committee at Coedpoeth paid visits to the free libraries at Hawarden and Chester to gain some ideas.[58] Provision was made for gas or electricity for lighting in most, if not all, of the libraries, which enabled them to open for long periods of time during the day to accommodate children of school age and adult workers. At Coedpoeth, for example, the reading room was open every day except Sunday, Good Friday and Christmas Day from 10 a.m. to 10 p.m.; the reference department was open from 10 a.m. until 8.30 p.m., and even the shorter hours of the lending department lasted from 11 a.m. to 1 p.m. and from 6 p.m. to 7.30 p.m. At Rhyl, the new building was heated with low-pressure hot-water apparatus and radiators. In short, all members of a community were catered for – which was of course part of Carnegie's philosophy.[59]

The terms of Carnegie's grants did not extend to the future management of the public libraries he sponsored, including the purchase of magazines and books. This, in Carnegie's view, was a legitimate charge on the rate income and any other resources available to local library committees, which, after all, should determine the nature of the reading materials placed in their libraries. While he himself rarely presented books to free and public libraries – still less to private institutions – he appreciated that some library committees were very limited in their capacity to buy books, though all made a point of subscribing to local newspapers (and there was a plethora of them available in the early twentieth century, in Welsh and in English) and to some magazines. Carnegie, however, encouraged the donation of books to the new libraries. One example of his personal intervention may have been the offer from the Smithsonian Institution in Washington to the library at Cricieth in 1907 of a selection of its publications.[60]

A far greater number of book donations were made by prominent social and political figures, including those who supported the foundation of Carnegie libraries in their own localities. Trecynon's library and public hall were opened in May 1903, the first public library in the Aberdare valley. It initially relied on 'well-wishers and friends', who presented 150 volumes, although a public subscription appeal had raised £180 the previous year.[61] At the opening of Coedpoeth's library in December 1904, a public advertisement seems to have been even more successful. It invited gifts of books, periodicals and pictures to supplement what could be bought with the limited resources available to the library; the printed catalogue of 1906 was put on sale at 3d a copy. However they were acquired, the library quickly sported a range of popular novels of quality by writers such as George Eliot, Mrs Gaskell, Daniel Defoe, Lewis Carroll, Harriet Beecher Stowe and the pioneering Welsh novelist from Flintshire Daniel Owen, who had died quite recently in 1895. Represented, too, were contemporary science books on coal mining and mine surveying which would have appealed to many in the mining communities of Coedpoeth and Bersham. Those with a taste for travel could read Lord Randolph Churchill's *Men, Mines and Animals of South Africa* (1892), while readers with a historical bent might borrow Pennant's *Tours in Wales* and the numerous books on local history by A. N. Palmer (died 1915), who had made his home in nearby Wrexham and after whom the local studies centre at Wrexham museum was later named. It was a swiftly acquired and varied collection of high literary and educational quality.[62]

At its opening on St David's Day in 1905, and in quite different social circumstances, the Carnegie library at Cricieth was presented with 130 books, and the ladies' committee of the library raised a further £22 8s. in a sale. Other gifts of books from individuals and religious societies followed to begin populating the shelving designed for 6,000 books, and so did some portraits for hanging in the library. At its opening, the deputy-lord lieutenant of Caernarfonshire, J. E. Greaves, whose family were slate-quarry owners and landowners in the county, expressed the social and educational ambitions of the borough for its new library:

the Institution was intended not only as a receptacle for literature but as a place for reasonable and rational social intercourse and recreation, where all might meet on equal terms, where political and sectarian divisions would be tabooed, and where all might enter and none be denied. (Cheers)[63]

At Whitchurch in 1905, soon after the library was opened, the approved recreation was less energetic: it was decided to set aside a table at the west end of the library for games 'as an experiment', the approved games being chess, draughts and dominoes.[64]

After opening the branch library at Dowlais in January 1907, D. A. Thomas, the industrialist and politician, was induced to give 100 guineas for the purchase of books a few months later.[65] The wife of Sir Samuel Thomas Evans, distinguished lawyer and politician and the Liberal MP for Mid Glamorgan since 1890, was invited to open the Coedfranc library at Skewen in June 1905, as a tribute to her husband's efforts in securing the Carnegie grant of £2,000. This was her first visit to Sir Samuel's birthplace, Neath, and on this occasion she not only presented the library with 150 books but also gave £100 for further purchases.[66] The village of Skewen was *en fête* for the occasion, and in his speech the MP himself exhorted those present to use their new library, not merely as a newspaper room, 'but as a place where they could obtain knowledge or food for the mind'. Perceptively, 'He considered there was a great difference between knowledge and information, and hoped they would read books that would elevate their minds and make them good citizens'. Presumably his wife's gifts assisted in this process.[67]

When the mayor of Newport opened the town's Corporation Road branch on 15 March 1907, he donated 100 books and took pride in being the first borrower from the lending library, choosing A. G. Bradley's popular book on the local historic environment, *In the March and Borderland of Wales*.[68] Abergavenny showed great determination and imagination in trying to stock the available shelving in its library. On 22 September 1905 Mr Wadbrook promised to donate the takings of his Royal Electrograph and Palace of Varieties in the town to the free library book fund. The net was cast more widely around the country and abroad, and promises flooded in, especially from clergymen willing to donate sermons and other ecclesiastical works – though the bishop of St David's declined to help and others preferred to visit the library before committing themselves. One may doubt whether this all-encompassing strategy produced quite what was appropriate in every case. The library's own funds enabled it to purchase a range of daily, weekly, monthly and quarterly newspapers and magazines of wide variety.[69]

The public enthusiasm and inventiveness of library committees in seeking to stock their libraries, if not necessarily their discrimination, matched the determination and pride of communities in their new free and public libraries. A number of the Carnegie libraries celebrated their establishment by publishing the catalogues of books which they had been able to acquire. At Flint a copy of the new *Flint Borough Catalogue* was presented to J. Herbert Lewis when he opened the library in 1903, and Wrexham published its extensive catalogue, extending to more than 150 pages, a year after the opening of its library in 1907. Within six years of its opening, even the small Carnegie library in the mining village of Abercanaid could boast a remarkably wide-ranging stock in its printed catalogue: 'Reference', 'Science Literature', 'General Literature' – encompassing history, travel, literature from Chaucer to the nineteenth century, and novels – as well as 'Theology' and a sizeable section on 'Welsh Literature'.[70]

PATRONS

Pride and determination were sentiments reflected in the choice of individuals to lay the foundation stones and to open formally the completed buildings. Prominent men and, occasionally, women with strong local attachments were invited and seem to have been enthusiastic in encouraging the public library movement. A number of notable Liberal politicians were among them. At Aberystwyth, the foundation stone was laid on 28 July 1905 by David Davies of Llandinam, soon to be the Liberal MP for Montgomeryshire. Andrew Carnegie was invited to open the library when completed; although he was unable to do so, he conveyed his personal wishes 'for the success of the Library and the happiness of all the people of Aberystwyth'.[71] The library was eventually opened in April 1906 by Mrs Vaughan Davies of Tanybwlch, the wife of Cardiganshire's Liberal MP, Matthew Lewis Vaughan Davies, whose sense of humour in a speech appealed to the spectators. An address by Principal T. F. Roberts of the University College of Wales amounted to a paean of praise to Aberystwyth as the pre-eminent centre of Welsh culture, with institutions – and a national library in prospect – that would now promote 'the higher life'.[72]

Figure 9. Crowds at the opening of Rhyl's library in April 1907. Among the dignitaries present was Sir J. Herbert Lewis MP (1858–1933), who is shown formally opening the library (Flintshire Record Office).

Coedpoeth's library was opened by Samuel Moss, the Liberal MP for Denbighshire East, on 12 December 1904, to loud cheers. In his speech, Moss declared education to be 'the foremost question of the day' and his own conviction that the great number of colliers in the district would use the library.[73] And at the opening of Colwyn Bay's library in April 1905, John Herbert Roberts, who had been the Liberal MP for Denbighshire West since 1892, was invited to give the address.[74] Further along the coast, the foundation stone of Rhyl's free library was laid in January 1906 by the high sheriff of Flintshire, W. J. P. Storye. The opening ceremony in April 1907 was presided over by the county's Liberal MP, J. Herbert Lewis, a lawyer and leading educationist, and a friend of Lloyd George; he declared that 'Henceforth every man and woman in the town of Rhyl, rich and poor, learned and unlearned, will own a library if not in their own houses, at least near their own doors'.[75]

In south Wales, D. A. Thomas, the Liberal MP for Merthyr Tydfil from 1888 to 1910, and an energetic industrialist, was in great demand when it came to opening Carnegie libraries, something which he approached with enthusiasm during the Edwardian years. Born near Aberdare, in August 1902 he laid the foundation stone of Trecynon's library and public hall, in the cross-party company of Lord Windsor of St Fagans, formerly president of the Library Association, which Thomas applauded. He took the chair at the opening of the building on 10 March 1903 and at the grand concert held to mark the occasion. In a wide-ranging speech on educational and cultural matters, he referred to the campaign for a National Museum for Wales and championed the idea that one university should be sufficient to serve the whole of Wales, which should not 'dissipate her forces by sub-division'.[76] No sooner had he laid the foundation stone at Trecynon, the first public library in the Aberdare valley, than he was at Penydarren to open its reading room on 20 September 1902, the first of the six branch libraries which Andrew Carnegie had recently agreed to sponsor in Merthyr's urban district. When he opened another branch, at Dowlais in January 1907, he presented 100 guineas for the purchase of books.[77]

The role of D. A. Thomas demonstrates how valuable in the promotion of public libraries was the advocacy of well-connected Liberal politicians in the influential circles in which Andrew Carnegie also moved. It was Thomas who seems to have presented the ambitious scheme for seven libraries in Merthyr's urban district to Carnegie in June 1902. Carnegie's secretary replied promptly and favourably from Skibo castle before the month was out, adding the millionaire's compliment to the Welsh people![78] Meanwhile, and further south, D. A. Thomas had been invited to open the new library at Church Village in September 1906, bringing to an end a decade of campaigning by the local community.[79]

Elsewhere, and reflecting perhaps the social attitudes of local authorities, some of the prominent gentry and titled nobility with whom they had a connection were sought as patrons of the new libraries. At Wrexham, for example, where the foundation stone of the library was laid by the mayoress on 1 January 1906, the completed building, with its large lecture hall, was opened on 15 February 1907 by the young Sir Foster Cunliffe of Acton Hall. He was a noted historian of the recent Boer War and, perhaps just

Figure 10. The plaque unveiled at the opening of Bangor's library by Lord Penrhyn in November 1907. It records Andrew Carnegie's gift of £2,500, along with £500 from Captain John Jones's legacy. It also notes the names of the chairman of the Museum, Bye-Laws and General Purposes Committee of the city council, Alderman W. P. Matthews, and the mayor, Col. Henry Platt C.B.

as much to the point, a first-class cricketer. His speech at the opening, in which he championed the cultural coexistence of English and Welsh, was laced with historical allusions.[80]

Bangor's library was opened in November 1907 by Lord Penrhyn, whose family had encouraged the library movement in the town in the past. In the south, Barry's library was opened on St David's Day 1906 by the lord lieutenant of Glamorgan, Lord Windsor, a major figure in the Library Association of Great Britain, who had recently been created earl of Plymouth. And while at Abergavenny the foundation stone was laid on 6 April 1905 by the mayor, Major W. Williams, who was also the energetic chairman of the library committee, no less a person than the marquess of Abergavenny formally opened the library in September 1906 – and welcomed Andrew Carnegie the following year when he received the freedom of the borough. It is not known whether all of these noble personages also contributed books from their own libraries, but at least when Lord Mostyn opened the new library at Llandudno in 1910, Sir Thomas Marchant Williams, lawyer, writer and a leading figure in the Honourable Society of Cymmrodorion in London, was present: his speech went out of its way to extol the importance of books and libraries.[81]

Lord Windsor of St Fagans, sometime president of the Library Association, could speak from experience and with feeling in September 1905 when he opened the new library in Penarth, whose site he had gifted to the town. He was well aware of some of the hostility in the country to establishing libraries at public cost, but he went out of his way to stress the benefits of reading – even of 'light literature'. He was reported as declaring that

> It was to provide opportunities for acquiring what he most fervently believed to be the highest form of literature that the foundations were laid in public libraries, and thus a taste for reading was cultivated which would be of immense value to those who took advantage of it. (Cheers)[82]

His words were echoed at Bridgend's opening ceremony on 30 August 1907, when a letter was read out from O. M. Edwards, the chief inspector of schools in Wales: 'There is no influence so undying as that of a good book'. No one would gainsay the opinion of the government's senior educational adviser for Wales.[83] As for the two new branch libraries in Cardiff, at Canton and Cathays, which the city's distinguished librarian John

Ballinger had patiently nursed from the original grant of £10,000 in 1903 to their opening on the same day in 1907, Andrew Carnegie took a particular interest in their building. He nominated his friend, Hew Morrison, to be his representative at the official ceremony when the Lord Mayor of Cardiff opened both buildings. Morrison (1849–1935) was no less distinguished than Ballinger as the chief librarian of the city of Edinburgh, who had, incidentally, interviewed James Bertram for the post of Carnegie's private secretary way back in 1898.[84]

EIGHT

ABORTIVE PROPOSALS FOR CARNEGIE LIBRARIES

THE CARNEGIE libraries of Wales took on average between two and five years to build, from the first appeal for a grant to the formal opening. Andrew Carnegie showed a patient, if unsentimental, understanding of the complexities of implementing the principles that underpinned his grants: the need for democratic approval, a readiness to adopt the Public Libraries Acts and to implement the penny rate, and the provision of a freehold site. Two of the smaller buildings, at Coedpoeth (or Bersham) and Rogerstone, took less than two years to build, and the libraries at Aberystwyth, Trecynon and Brynmawr not much longer. Where the negotiations were prolonged, the question of a freehold site was most often the explanation. Where they proved abortive, despite the offer of grants from Carnegie, the reasons were often more complex.

Carnegie's eagerness to encourage the foundation of free, public libraries was matched by alert individuals who were ambitious for their own communities to seize the opportunity of his philanthropy to erect buildings which, in small towns or industrial villages, might be the only notable public building available to the community at large. In all parts of Wales it is noticeable that the first steps were taken by several local authorities within a year or so of Carnegie's vision becoming widely known. It was inevitable that a number of issues arose which either delayed or undermined the discussions that followed. James Bertram, on behalf of Carnegie, showed commendable patience in dealing with them over the following decade – issues that arose from the broad principles of Carnegie's library philanthropy and which proved more troublesome in some districts than in others: the question of a site, popular opinion especially towards a potential increase in the rates, authorities' preferences, the speed of negotiations, and so on.

The relatively small number of Welsh towns which had already established free, public libraries in the later decades of the nineteenth century, before the coffers of Andrew Carnegie were thrown open, did not qualify for his grants. They already devoted the penny rate to their maintenance and, like Swansea, Newport and Cardiff, had been able to finance impressive, purpose-built buildings. Nevertheless, Carnegie was open to proposals for the establishment of branch libraries in these towns, in place of rented accommodation. However, similar issues to those confronted elsewhere had to be addressed. Following lengthy discussions between Cardiff's town council and Andrew Carnegie, on 26 August 1903 James Bertram was able to confirm that Carnegie would meet the cost of building two new branch libraries in the working-class districts of Canton and Cathays, as the council proposed, up to a total sum of £10,000. Apart from the usual stipulations, Carnegie noted that his grant should be in addition to the present library rate, which already supported the central library and several existing branch libraries, and that the town council would need to find £1,000 per annum for the maintenance of the two new libraries. The council accepted the terms of this grant in short order.[1]

Similarly, Newport already had two branch libraries before it planned another, in Corporation Road, on the eastern side of the river Usk, in 1905. For this building, the borough council appealed to Andrew Carnegie for aid and he promised £2,000. The total cost, including heating and electric lighting, had been pared down to £2,000 12s. 1d by the time the library was opened by the mayor in March 1907.[2]

At Swansea, discussions with Carnegie were under way by October 1902, and it was made clear to the council that an extra halfpenny rate would need to be levied beyond what was spent on the imposing central library opened by W. E. Gladstone in 1889. The town already had six branch libraries in leased accommodation, and it was hoped that between £10,000 and £15,000 would be forthcoming to build permanent libraries. Several promises of freehold sites had been secured, including from the earl of Jersey as a major landowner in eastern Swansea. Following Carnegie's offer of £8,000 early in 1904, the Beaumont Thomas of Cwmbwrla works offered a site nearby, and it was hoped that Vivian and Sons, Swansea's pre-eminent industrial firm, would be prepared to offer one at Brynhyfryd, overlooking their large works. But the entire plan came to nothing when a poll of ratepayers rejected the Carnegie offer, largely as a result of resistance to the extra halfpenny rate, though reference was also made in the council to the Homestead strike in 1892 which still lingered in the memory of industrial communities.[3]

A formal scheme for four branch libraries to serve Swansea's five wards was finally accepted in 1904. Messrs Thomas had offered a freehold site at Cwmbwrla, and Vivian and Sons one at Landore; a private subscription was expected to raise enough for a new library at Morriston. The recommendation that a library for St Helen's ward should be built at the entrance to Victoria Park presumably depended on the council itself making the site available. The only reservation, communicated by James Bertram to the council, made clear that Carnegie's grant could not extend to an art gallery, a museum or an extension to the central library: that might result in starving the branches of essential resources from the rates. On 21 October 1903 the council gratefully accepted these terms for the grant. On 4 November James Bertram, showing some flexibility, in his turn accepted the council's scheme, in a letter from New York.[4] It is not certain that any of the proposed Carnegie branch libraries was built at this juncture, and certainly the question of a site at Morriston was still under discussion in the summer of 1904. The last communication between Swansea and Carnegie on the entire subject took place at the beginning of 1905.[5]

Elsewhere, a number of proposed libraries never materialized despite a successful appeal to Carnegie for funding. He was ready to respond positively to enquiries from local authorities and individuals, most notably from the upper reaches of the mining valleys of the south Wales coalfield. What his reaction was – or might have been – to a suggested enquiry from the workmen's library and institute committee at Tredegar, a major early iron-making and latterly a coal-mining town, is unknown. The library and institute, founded in 1890, were supported by weekly contributions from the workmen, and they were housed in the Temperance Hall 'on suffrance' from a public company, the Temperance Society and its trustees. In July 1902 the committee considered a proposal to approach Andrew Carnegie for a sum of money that would enable it to build a library of its own in the

town. Such a proposal would have run contrary to the principles govern-
ing Carnegie's library grants: it did not come from a local authority which
had adopted the Public Libraries Act and therefore would have access to
the penny rate, and there was the question of a freehold site. The committee may have realized this at an early stage and as far as is known no
approach to Carnegie ever took place.[6]

Even among some of the recipients of his bounty, occasional misgivings were expressed. The condition attached to his grants whereby
communities were expected to maintain the new buildings could be
observed more easily in substantial towns than in smaller communities, some of whose applications for funds were consequently rejected
or the funding proved inadequate in the longer term. At Panteg, near
Pontypool, where there was a large steelworks, Councillor F. W. Harding of New Inn had taken the initiative to propose to Andrew Carnegie
that libraries be established at the villages of Griffithstown, New Inn
and either Cwm or Pontymoile, within the urban district. For his part,
Carnegie was prepared to look favourably on a proposal to fund a library
building in a central location in the urban district rather than in three
separate ones, mainly because the penny rate would yield only £103 per
annum and a site would need to be made available for any building that
was built with Carnegie funds. 'It is idle to suggest three libraries where
the revenue will not keep one going properly', his secretary explained.
Nevertheless, when Panteg's urban district council considered the matter further in November 1903, Councillor Harding persisted with his
proposal for three libraries and sought to assure Carnegie that sufficient
annual income would be forthcoming from somewhere; there the matter seems to have rested, with no further response from Carnegie on
this occasion.[7]

The difficulty at Panteg was replicated not far away in Abersychan's
urban district, in the Afon Lwyd valley north-west of Pontypool. There,
early in 1903, Andrew Carnegie made a substantial grant of £3,000 available for three public libraries, provided (as usual) sites were acquired
and the Public Libraries Act was adopted, resulting in a revenue stream
of £200 per annum to maintain the buildings.[8] Carnegie envisaged the
libraries being built at Garndiffaith and Pontnewynydd, as well as at
Abersychan itself, but that would have excluded the community at Varteg. Local inhabitants recognized that it would not be advisable to divide
the £1,000 for Garndiffaith so as to accommodate Varteg's needs, and so
the council resolved to make a further appeal to Andrew Carnegie on

Varteg's behalf. Other difficulties also arose. It was anticipated that the industrialist John Capel Hanbury of Pontypool Park would be likely to provide only two of the freehold sites required, and in any case Abersychan's plans extended to incorporating 'public offices' and a caretaker's house on the site of its public library, while the people of Pontnewynydd sought to build a public hall over the proposed library – which doubtless increased Carnegie's unease. The discussions reached a stalemate.[9] Instead, the nearby town of Pontypool decided to approach Andrew Carnegie separately, and in December 1904 he agreed to offer £2,000 for a new and more centrally situated library for the entire area. A year later, John Capel Hanbury offered a site in the very centre of Pontypool, near his own mansion and opposite the police station, and in 1908 he formally opened the new building.[10]

A similar situation in some respects occurred at Caerphilly, though with a less positive outcome for the area. As the centre of railway works and a focus of the coal industry in eastern Glamorgan, the urban district included five wards. The chamber of commerce and the workmen's institute library committee coordinated an appeal to Andrew Carnegie for a grant on the usual terms. In March 1905, he agreed to provide £3,000 towards the creation of three libraries, reasoning that the anticipated revenue from the rates (£290) was not sufficient to maintain a library in all five wards. Caerphilly urban district council considered Carnegie's proposal on 4 April 1905 and the workmen's institute agreed to hand over its books if it were accepted. The council, however, resolved to ask Carnegie if he would give an additional grant to enable a library to be established in each of the five wards or, failing that, to commit to provide the extra £2,000 needed so that when the proceeds of the penny rate reached £500, two other libraries could be built. It was an audacious suggestion arising out of the council's own dilemma: it was sensitive to the costs of travel if only three libraries were built, and to the implication that the population of two wards would be asked to contribute to the penny rate when they had no library of their own. Although it did not consult the electorate of ratepayers, the council on 26 February 1906 resolved to reject Carnegie's offer. There was dissatisfaction with this decision, in both the chamber of commerce and the town of Caerphilly, and the 'Library Question' dragged on. It was suggested, with some ingenuity, that books might be circulated by arrangement around the five wards if only three libraries were built, so that, as one councillor put it in March 1906, 'our young people may have every facility for reading the best books and thereby equip themselves to fight the battle of life'. But the council was not persuaded, and only in 1910 was a further approach made to Andrew Carnegie. In June of that year, his secretary replied that the original offer was still open on the same terms, but the council was again divided; despite a reminder from James Bertram in July of the following year, no further action was taken, and no library was built with Carnegie funds in Caerphilly or its wards.[11] Local interests and differences of opinion, including among councillors, rather than a refusal by Carnegie to breach his principles of philanthropy when other requests continued to flood his postbag, were responsible for delaying the building of a library at Caerphilly.[12]

Carnegie himself rejected several other and more modest requests at the initial stage, usually because he concluded that the ambitions went beyond the capacity of the local authority to fulfil them. At Llanidloes in 1902, for example, he judged that the income from the penny rate was wholly inadequate to support a new library. Indeed, the costs of upkeep even where new libraries were sponsored by Carnegie were to be a recurring headache for small authorities which tried to develop their services. He reportedly offered £1,500 for a new library at Connah's Quay in Flintshire in the summer of 1903, on condition that the council raised a further £600 to sustain it. Despite the council's enthusiasm, the opportunity was missed.[13]

Similarly, at both Machynlleth and Cricieth it was apparent that even with a Carnegie grant the authority would also need to establish a maintenance fund of its own over and above the proceeds of the annual penny rate. At Machynlleth, a small market town at the head of the Dyfi estuary, the eventual outcome was sunnier. As early as November 1902, a public meeting was held to consider Carnegie's intimation that he would respond positively to a request for a grant for a public library in the town. Where the original approach had come from is unclear, though it may have been prompted by the young David Davies of Llandinam, the politician and philanthropist who became MP for Montgomeryshire in 1906 and who later proved a notable supporter of Carnegie libraries. However, after further consideration of the details of Machynlleth's proposal, James Bertram replied from New York on 17 December 1902 that it was unlikely that Carnegie would offer more than £1,000 when the rates of the town could muster only £35 per annum to support a new library. The town would need to raise a further £1,000 itself for the proposal to be viable and the library sustainable. There the matter rested following a further public meeting in January 1903, until David Davies himself presented the town in 1911 with not only a site for a new library, but also a refurbished late fifteenth-century building, the Owen Glendower Institute, which would house the town's library and other amenities for long after.[14]

At Aberaman, a mining village between Aberdare and Mountain Ash, Carnegie's offer of £1,000 for a new library was accepted at a meeting held on 4 October 1902 and negotiations were begun with local landowners for a site. Eventually the Powell Dyffryn Company offered a site for a combined hall and library in July 1904. But by the time the plans were submitted to Andrew Carnegie in the autumn of 1906 they had mushroomed into a proposal for a hall and an institute as well as a library. This again sounded alarm bells for Carnegie, whose response from Skibo castle on 3 October reminded the council that he had offered £1,000 for a library, which now seemed to be a small part of the current plan. Shortly afterwards, the council withdrew from the negotiations.[15]

Further south in the Cynon valley, just to the north of Pontypridd, which already had a free, public library, Carnegie evidently offered to fund the building of three new libraries in the neighbouring settlements of Abercynon, Penrhiwceiber and Ynysybwl; but early in October 1902 this offer was rejected on the grounds that it would disadvantage the workmen of Mountain Ash, who were already paying a levy for their miners' library.[16]

Indeed, the existence in Glamorgan and Monmouthshire of a score and more of miners' libraries, funded by levies on the workmen themselves, was an added complication where the authorities yearned for a Carnegie grant. They were subscription libraries and although they might often be opened to a wider membership among trades and professional people – known as 'outsiders' – it was only later that women and children were universally admitted, perhaps after the example of public libraries like those funded by Andrew Carnegie.[17]

Although relations with the workmen's organization were cooperative enough in Caerphilly, the same was not true everywhere. The miners' institutes and welfare hall libraries valued their independence and often scorned would-be benefactors. More than thirty libraries or reading rooms had opened, mainly during the 1880s and 1890s, many of them associated with workmen's halls or miners' institutes, and they continued to be established in the Edwardian years. They provided social amenities apart from libraries. There was also reluctance to adopt the Public Libraries Act and a commitment to payment of a penny rate when miners, doubtless ratepayers among them, were already contributing to their own institutes and libraries. However, a few communities – like Treharris – did succeed in establishing both a workmen's library and a Carnegie-sponsored free, public library.[18]

Further west, in the anthracite sector of the south Wales coalfield, north-west of Swansea, a grant was sought from Andrew Carnegie by the parish council of Llandeilo-Talybont on behalf of Pontarddulais and the smaller village of Gorseinon.The sum suggested may have exceeded what he considered appropriate, for on 2 September 1902 Bertram's letter from Skibo castle noted that Carnegie had already approved grants of £700 for local libraries in Mountain Ash, Aberdare and Merthyr districts (though not all of these materialized in the event) and that'modest buildings of the same nature' at the same cost would be more appropriate for both Pontarddulais and Gorseinon.[19] A week or so later, the council discussed the letter and accepted its terms, although Gorseinon was reported to be more enthusiastic than Pontarddulais, where there remained some opposition and the question of a freehold site also needed to be resolved.[20] There was too a misunderstanding at Skibo castle – even a suspicion of sharp practice – which led to a further letter from Carnegie on 17 October. This reminded the council that the original appeal for funds had been on the basis of a penny rate of £80 per annum for each library rather than a total of £80 for the two, as had evidently emerged in recent exchanges. Carnegie judged that the latter was not adequate to sustain two libraries without another 'assured and permanent source', rather than an additional levy of a penny imposed on each workman, who might already be supporting another library in the district. That brought the discussion about Carnegie libraries at Pontarddulais and Gorseinon to an abrupt end.[21]

Much more leisurely, but no more productive, were the negotiations between Carnegie and the town of Brecon, which took a very long time. Well before Carnegie came on the scene, in 1896 a proposal to establish a public library in Brecon to celebrate QueenVictoria's forthcoming Diamond Jubilee was made by John Lloyd, a local philanthropist and London lawyer.The idea, which gained local support, mirrored one that was popular in other substantial towns, namely that Brecon's literary institute, which had been established in 1874, should be the nucleus of a new public library. Seven years later, in July 1903, Carnegie offered a grant of £3,000 for a library in the town of Brecon and, unusually, also

£5,000 for a library to serve the rural parts of the county – an arrangement that prefigured the later change in the direction of Carnegie's British philanthropy. But the insistence that the penny rate should be imposed in both town and county caused lengthy heart-searching in Brecon. In March 1904 Carnegie agreed that his offer should be kept open for 'a reasonable period', but in the event the county council resolved to reject the offer in 1910.[22]

NINE

THE CARNEGIE
LEGACY IN WALES

IN TERMS OF buildings, the thirty-five known Carnegie libraries – all but one of which still stand today – are Andrew Carnegie's tangible legacy in Wales. The educational and cultural purposes to which they have been put during the past century are his intangible legacy. Yet there are two other associated ways in which his philanthropy has left its indelible mark on Welsh society.

Carnegie's earliest philanthropic projects, most notably in education, reflected personal interests that were maintained from an early stage in his life. Although he had never been to university himself, he later on, in 1901, gave $10 million to the Carnegie Trust for Universities in Scotland. The four Scottish universities (St Andrews, Glasgow, Aberdeen and Edinburgh), founded in the fifteenth and sixteenth centuries and with a long international scientific and cultural reputation, were much admired by Carnegie; he took a regular personal interest in their affairs and they have continued to benefit handsomely from his benefactions. Wales's three non-sectarian institutions of higher education, created in the last quarter of the nineteenth century, seemed of a different order in Carnegie's day. Aberystwyth, Bangor and Cardiff – and the University of Wales which incorporated them in 1893 – had barely got off the ground by 1900, and an appeal to Carnegie for financial support by Lord Rendel, Aberystwyth's president, in 1901, was not successful, even though Rendel had been a

Liberal MP and a friend of Mr Gladstone.[1] However, it may be added that in 1926 the Carnegie Trust offered the single largest initial gift of £2,500 to facilitate the establishment of the pioneering and independent adult education college Coleg Harlech the following year, with the aim of extending adult education at a higher level.[2]

Manifestly, it was education for the mass of the population which counted most for Andrew Carnegie, and his two other such projects left a legacy in Wales as elsewhere. His sponsorship of church and chapel pipe organs began in the early 1870s, probably in 1873, even before his plans to support library buildings began to be formulated, and eventually this sponsorship resulted in contributions to the purchase of at least 7,689 organs throughout North America and the United Kingdom – almost three times the number of libraries he sponsored – and, it may be noted, this included more than 1,000 organs in Scotland alone. During his lifetime, he spent over $1,500,000 on more than 3,000 organs in England and Scotland: 2,119 in England, 1,005 in Scotland and hundreds more elsewhere.

In Wales, at least thirty-two organs were paid for in whole or in part by Andrew Carnegie, costing at least $22,210. James Bertram was given charge of the organ programme in 1898 and he dealt with numerous requests as he did those for library grants. Carnegie appreciated full well that most working men and their families were likely to be introduced to classical and sacred music in a religious setting, as Carnegie himself had been in the nonconformist household in which he grew up. His father, who died when Andy was twenty, was a member of the Swedenborgian Church in Scotland and in Pennsylvania, where the sect was concentrated. The son was not a spiritually minded man, and in making his donations to organs he did not discriminate between denominations at a time when many churches and chapels were being rebuilt in Wales. He installed a large organ in his own palatial residence in New York, and later in life, at Skibo castle, he and his guests would rise to a morning organ performance.[3]

As with his library benefactions, Carnegie expected churches and chapels which sought his help to raise part of the cost of the new instruments – usually a half – themselves. His gifts for the purchase of organs were not confined to towns or communities in which he supported new libraries. It is true that when, in October 1904, he offered £1,500 for a new library building for the mining community of Coedpoeth, not far from Wrexham, he also offered £200 towards the installation of an organ at Rehoboth Welsh Wesleyan Methodist Church in the village, on condition that a further £200 were raised by its members. And at Wrexham itself, he donated £150 for a new organ for Queen Street Congregational Church in October 1906. At Swansea, where negotiations for several new Carnegie branch libraries had recently come to grief, he sent a cheque for £150 to Mr Warmington of Swansea market in November 1906 to pay off the debt on the new organ bought for the Bible Christian Chapel in Oxford Street.[4]

At the same time, Carnegie welcomed applications from Welsh- and English-speaking congregations of churches and chapels in rural as well as more urbanized districts. In September 1905 the vicar of Milford Haven was delighted to receive news that Carnegie would contribute half the total cost of £600 for a new organ for St Katherine's Church, which was about to be enlarged. The following year he part-funded a new organ for the parish church of Llanraeadr-ym-Mochnant, west of Oswestry; it was dedicated , presumably with Carnegie's knowledge, to the memory of a former vicar of the church, Dr William Morgan, who had translated the Bible into Welsh in the 1580s.[5] Moreover, in the large iron and steel town of Llanelli, whose public library pre-dated the Carnegie programme, Capel Newydd, one of the best known and finest chapel buildings in Wales, inaugurated a grand pipe organ in 1912 to mark the completion of the chapel's renovation; Andrew Carnegie paid half the cost of £600 for that new instrument.[6]

Two chapels in the slate-shipping port of Port Dinorwic on the Menai Strait attracted Carnegie grants: Shiloh Chapel was reported to have received a large donation of £300 towards a new organ in February 1907, while two and a half years later the Wesleyan Chapel was promised £100 to defray half the cost of its new organ. Not far along the coast, Caernarfon, which already had a pre-Carnegie public library, was reported on 8 February 1907 to have received a donation of £300 for another new organ. And at Barmouth, on the Merioneth coast, the new organ of the English Presbyterian Church attracted a £125 grant from Carnegie in October 1906.[7] Taking some examples in industrial south Wales, the Primitive Methodist Church at Risca received a modest £125 for a pipe organ from Carnegie, as reported on 19 March 1910. And about the same time, the renovated organ at the Calvinistic Methodist Church in Blaenavon, costing £130, accepted a contribution of £100 from Carnegie.[8]

Carnegie's dedicated commitment to provide libraries and organs for the general public extended well beyond his own lifetime. The Carnegie Corporation of New York was set up in 1911 with Andrew Carnegie as its president and chairman, and James Bertram as its secretary, in order to manage henceforward much of his general philanthropy. It was followed by the companion Carnegie United Kingdom Trust in October 1913, which had a separate administrative structure. Within two or three years the latter had assumed responsibility for the library and organ benefactions, which had grown in number somewhat haphazardly. Moreover, in retirement Andrew Carnegie's mind became increasingly preoccupied by the cause of international peace from 1910 onwards, the year in which the Carnegie Endowment for International Peace was created, and this preoccupation became all the stronger as tensions in Europe rose. This aspect of his philanthropy was directed towards establishing institutions to resolve international disputes and heralded the movement for the League of Nations after the Great War ended. The Peace Palace at The Hague had opened in 1913 with $1.5 million donated by Carnegie; it was intended to house the Permanent Court of Arbitration to work for peace and to limit weapons development.[9]

As far as libraries in the United Kingdom are concerned, the framework for the redirection of his philanthropy was provided, first, by a report which the Carnegie United Kingdom Trust commissioned soon after its establishment. W. G. S. Adams was a fellow Scot and an academic who developed a close connection with the United States. By 1913 he was Gladstone professor of political theory and institutions at Oxford, and his interest in internationalism also commended him to Carnegie and the Trust, which engaged him to survey the state of library services throughout the United Kingdom, in town and countryside alike. Adams produced his detailed and thorough report in 1915. Then, after the end of the war, in 1919 county councils were given a statutory right to establish library services throughout their counties, something which the Trust committed itself to supporting as an extension of Carnegie's personal benefactions from the more populous communities to include more rural areas. The Library Association and politicians like Lord Windsor and J. Herbert Lewis, who had long shared some of Carnegie's ideals in public education, were instrumental in achieving these changes.[10]

The mainspring of Carnegie's distribution of funds for libraries and organs had not initially been to direct or regulate their expenditure in detail, but this changed after the assessment undertaken by Professor Adams and following Carnegie's own death in 1919. Although libraries remained a major undertaking of the Carnegie United Kingdom Trust, the earlier policy of not buying books for the new Carnegie libraries and of maintaining the buildings once they had been built – something which Carnegie had regarded as the responsibility of the local communities themselves through the rates and local philanthropy – was significantly modified. Thus, the Trust gradually transformed and developed his initial vision into a library service, rather than a network of buildings, that would encompass the whole country, including Wales, giving priority to less wealthy and less urbanized communities.[11]

The practice of making individual library building grants was phased out after 1913. Moreover, it was realized that much of sparsely populated and rural Wales (and, indeed, of the United Kingdom generally) was still remote from a free, public library. The brief of the Carnegie United Kingdom Trust now encompassed 'the well-being of the masses of the people of Great Britain and Ireland', taking over responsibility from the parent Carnegie Corporation of New York and continuing to support libraries and the purchase of organs, but in a much broader and coordinated geographical context. It embarked on the sponsorship of 'county libraries' throughout the kingdom. The aim of the county schemes was to circulate books to villages from a central repository, using local schools, even pubs and hotels, rather than to continue financing individual library buildings. The grants could henceforward be spent on books and salaries and, through the schools, serve the younger readers in scattered locations. Carnegie library building works which were underway in 1913 had come to an end by November 1917, by which time the Carnegie United Kingdom Trust was fully functioning and had embarked on the new policy. Requests which had elicited promises of funding were usually terminated, as John Lloyd, who had approached Carnegie on behalf of the town and county of Brecon as early as 1903, could testify. He received the following firm but courteous letter from Carnegie in New York on 18 December 1913 – sent, one suspects, more in regret and disappointment than in anger:

> Having transferred the administration of the funds made available by me for the erection of Public Libraries and the procuring of Church Organs, within the United Kingdom, to the Carnegie United Kingdom Trustees, who transact the business of their Trust in my native town of Dunfermline, I beg to state that all applications for grants for the foregoing purposes will hereafter be disposed of by them, and that my offer, made in 1903 of a grant in response to a request from you, on behalf of Town and County of Breckon [sic] not having been taken advantage of after the lapse of several years must now be held as recalled.[12]

The first of the county libraries to be established was in Staffordshire, in 1915. In Wales, negotiations were afoot so that by the time the Public Libraries Act was passed in 1919, six counties had either received or been

Figure 11. Andrew Carnegie's daughter Margaret (1897–1990) photo-graphed with her husband, Roswell Miller Jr (1894–1983), on the occasion of their visit to Aberystwyth's library in July 1921 (Ceredigion Archives).

promised financial help with their rural schemes. The first two were among Wales's most sparsely populated counties. Negotiations began with Caer-narfonshire in 1916 and eventually it started its county library scheme in October 1918, possibly with the encouragement of Lloyd George, whose brother, William George, became the county library committee's first chairman. Cardiganshire, which had only one Carnegie library, built in Aberystwyth, followed in September 1919, just a few weeks after the death of Carnegie himself. The illness of Andrew Carnegie's daughter Margaret had prevented her father from visiting the National Eisteddfod at Caernarfon in 1906, but in 1921 Margaret and her husband, Roswell Miller, took an interest in Cardiganshire's new scheme, and while both were still in their twenties they visited Aberystwyth and its library in 1921.[13]

As had often been the case with proposals for the establishment of Carnegie's libraries in Wales, the Trust's negotiations with the Welsh county authorities did not run smoothly; especially intractable was the situation in Glamorgan, where resistance to the Public Libraries Act of 1919 from Rhondda and Mountain Ash urban district councils continued into the 1930s, partly because of the flourishing miners' institutes and libraries, and partly because of the costs that might be involved. By that date, however, Carnegie's stamp on the public library movement in Wales as a whole was indelible: it deserves to be recalled and recorded.[14]

Figure 12. Andrew Carnegie's daughter Margaret and her husband (second row, centre) photographed with the library committee inside Aberystwyth's well-stocked library during their visit in July 1921. Also in the photograph (third row, second left) is John Ballinger (1860–1933), who was influential in creating Carnegie libraries in Cardiff and Glamorgan and became the first librarian of the National Library of Wales in 1908 (Ceredigion Archives).

NOTES

1. THE PUBLIC LIBRARY

1. See Catherine Bennett, 'Comment and Analysis', *The Observer*, 13 January 2019, for the quotation.
2. By contrast, see A. Grimes, *Irish Carnegie Libraries: A Catalogue and Architectural History* (Dublin, 1998), which lists, with illustrations, more than sixty Irish libraries, and discusses their planning, architecture and management.
3. Simon Jenkins, *The Guardian*, 22 December 2016.
4. For libraries as sources of inspiration, see *The Big Issue*, 12–18 November 2018.

2. ANDREW CARNEGIE, 1835–1919

1. G. Tweedale, 'Andrew Carnegie (1835–1919)', in H. C. G. Matthew (ed.), *Oxford Dictionary of National Biography* (Oxford, 2004), and *http://www. oxforddnb.com*; J. F. Wall, 'Andrew Carnegie', in J. A. Garraty and M. C. Carnes (eds), *American National Biography* (24 vols, New York and Oxford, 1999), vol. 4, pp. 408–15. Among a number of biographies of Carnegie, see especially B. J. Hendrick, *The Life of Andrew Carnegie* (London, 1932); J. F. Wall, *Andrew Carnegie*, 2nd edn (Pittsburgh, 1989); J. Mackay, *Little Boss: A Life of Andrew Carnegie* (Edinburgh and London, 1997); and D. Nasaw, *Andrew Carnegie* (London, 2006).

2. See A. M. Hacker, *The World of Andrew Carnegie, 1865–1901* (Philadelphia and New York, 1968), pp. 337–62, for a case study of Carnegie's career as an entrepreneur and its basis in the iron and steel industries.
3. Hendrick, *The Life of Andrew Carnegie*, ch. 27; Tweedale, 'Andrew Carnegie (1835–1919)', *ODNB, s.n.* The Carnegies had one daughter, Margaret (1897–1990). For his purchase of Skibo castle, see S. Goodenough, *The Greatest Good Fortune: Andrew Carnegie's Gift for Today* (Edinburgh, 1985), pp. 270–3.

3.   PHILANTHROPY AND THE FREE LIBRARY

1. *North American Review*, CXLVIII (June 1889) and CXLIX (December 1889); A. Carnegie, *The Gospel of Wealth and Other Timely Essays*, ed. E. C. Kirkland (Cambridge, MA, 1965), with this essay reprinted as ch. 2 (pp. 14–48). The quotations that follow are taken from this edition of 'Wealth'.
2. *The Gospel of Wealth*, ed. Kirkland, p. 68, for this later essay.
3. *Barry Dock News*, 1 January 1904.
4. *Cardiff Times*, 21 November 1903, 20 October 1906.
5. *The Cambria Daily Leader*, 8 April 1914. It should be noted that the Homestead clash in 1892 occurred when Carnegie himself was in Scotland.
6. See Wall, *Andrew Carnegie*, pp. 806–15, for criticism of 'The Gospel of Wealth'; for the myth of the 'Robber Barons', see Hacker, *World of Andrew Carnegie*, pp. xvii–xxii, and M. Klein, *The Change Makers: From Carnegie to Gates, How the Great Entrepreneurs Transformed Ideas into Industries* (New York, 2003), pp. 1–17 (Prologue: 'Say Good-bye to the Robber Barons'), pp. 246–8.
7. See, for example, C. Harvey, H. Maclean, J. Gordon and E. Shaw, 'Andrew Carnegie and the foundations of contemporary entrepreneurial philanthropy', *Business History*, 53/3 (2011), 425–50, on 'entrepreneurial philanthropy' and its capacity for 'world-making' in cultural, social and symbolic spheres; and, by contrast, A. Giridharadas, *Winners Take All* (London, 2019).
8. Hendrick, *The Life of Andrew Carnegie*, p. 542.
9. For his debt to Col. Anderson and his 'free lending library' in 1853, see Mackay, *Little Boss*, pp. 63–4; Wall, *Andrew Carnegie*, pp. 106–8; and Nasaw, *Andrew Carnegie*, pp. 42–3.
10. Quoted by John Harris in *The Guardian*, 15 December 2017.
11. Nasaw, *Andrew Carnegie*, p. 193. See Hacker, *The World of Andrew Carnegie*, pp. 363–73, and Goodenough, *The Great Good Fortune*, pp. 3–10, for the influences on him and the importance he attached to education. For a brief, frank autobiography, see *The Youth's Companion*, 23 April 1896, repr. in J. C. van

Dyke (ed.), *Autobiography of Andrew Carnegie* (New York, 1920, 2006), and in *The Gospel of Wealth*, ed. Kirkland, ch. 1.

12. Wall, *Andrew Carnegie*, pp. 212, 354; A. Thompson, *Library Buildings of Britain and Europe* (London, 1963), p. 74.

4. EARLY PUBLIC LIBRARIES IN WALES

1. J. Roe, 'The Public Library in Wales: its history and development in the context of local government' (unpublished MA thesis, Queen's University Belfast, 1970), ch. 1, especially 7–33. This valuable study has never been published. For some key episodes in this early story more generally, see A. Crawford (ed.), *The Meaning of the Library: A Cultural History* (Princeton and Oxford, 2015), pp. 110–13, 126.

2. The first Library Act of 1850 was extended to Scotland in 1855, giving town corporations the authority to levy the tax on local ratepayers. See, in general, T. Kelly, *History of Public Libraries in Great Britain, 1845–1975* (London, 1977).

3. P. F. Tobin, 'Pontypridd Public Library, 1890–1990', in P. F. Tobin and J. I. Davies (eds), *The Bridge and the Song: Some Chapters in the Story of Pontypridd* (Bridgend, 1991), pp. 66–77 (p. 67). For the impact of the Acts generally in Wales, see P. H. Jones, 'Public libraries in Wales since 1862', in A. Black and P. Hoare (eds), *The Cambridge History of Libraries in Britain and Ireland* (Cambridge, 2006), pp. 216–26.

4. In 1863 Llanelli's mechanics' institute had 1,651 books on a wide range of subjects – history, religion, science, art, commerce, law, politics and literature (including in Welsh, the habitual language of the town's inhabitants); its reading room had daily papers, six weekly Welsh publications and five monthlies. See J. Edwards, *Llanelli: Story of a Town* (for *The Llanelli Star*, Derby, 2001).

5. C. Briggs, '"Carnegie offered money and a lot of south Wales refused to have it: it was blood money": Bringing public libraries to the south Wales valleys, 1870–1939', *Library History*, 17 (November 2001), 171–9, which concentrates on western Monmouthshire and eastern Glamorgan.

6. Unless otherwise stated, see Roe, 'The Public Library in Wales', 34–67, for details of these libraries.

7. Ceredigion Archives, ABM/SE/1/5, pp. 582–3, 586. For a brief account of the early years of the free public library, see W. J. Lewis, *Born on a Perilous Rock: Aberystwyth Past and Present* (Aberystwyth, 1980), 183–4.

8. S. Awbery, *Let Us Talk of Barry* ([Barry], 1954), pp. 91–2; D. Moore (ed.), *Barry: The Centenary Book* (Barry, 1984; 2nd rev. edn 1988), p. 186.

9. Even in 1906 Aberystwyth's penny rate was estimated to bring in only £180 per annum: *Cambrian News and Merionethshire Standard*, 27 April 1906.
10. Gwent Archives, Abergavenny Borough Council, D894/19, pp. 457–61, 490–1.
11. For these figures, see Mackay, *Little Boss*, pp. 255, 264; Wall, *Andrew Carnegie*, pp. 836–7; and Nasaw, *Andrew Carnegie*, p. 607. See also Hendrick, *The Life of Andrew Carnegie*, pp. 547–57, for Carnegie's sponsorship of libraries in general.

5. ANDREW CARNEGIE AND WALES

1. Wall, *Andrew Carnegie*, pp. 314–16; Mackay, *Little Boss*, pp. 148–50, 161–2. The Jones family's emigration from Brecon is noted in *The Cambrian*, 10/4 (April 1890), 98, a reference I owe to Bill Jones's namesake, Professor W. D. Jones.
2. Quoted in Nasaw, *Andrew Carnegie*, p. 167.
3. *The Evening Express*, 9 May 1903, which also carried a report of the life of Bill Jones and of the circumstances of his death in 1889.
4. For an estimate of Jones's importance to the Carnegie company, see Wall, *Andrew Carnegie*, pp. 344, 358–9, 519–22, 532–4; for the thousands who lined Pittsburgh's streets at Jones's public funeral, see Mackay, *Little Boss*, p. 185. A 'family memoir', written by T. Gage, Captain Jones's great-grandson, *American Prometheus: Carnegie's Captain, Bill Jones* (Arcata, CA, 2017), takes a more jaundiced view of relations between Jones's family and Carnegie after the captain's death.
5. For Thomas's visit to the USA, see R. W. Burnie (ed.), *Memoir and Letters of Sidney Gilchrist Thomas, Inventor* (London, 1891), ch. 13, esp. pp. 147–8, 151–2, 154–5, based in large part on his letters. Thomas may have encountered Jones in Britain in November 1878 when, as he wrote to a cousin, 'I see a good deal of Americans just now. I have struck up an alliance with one I encountered abroad' (pp. 127–8).
6. For the quotations, see *Memoirs and Letters*, pp. 157–8, and J. Knight, *Blaenavon: From Iron Town to World Heritage Site* (Wooton Almeley, 2016), ch. 8, esp. pp. 107–14 ('Sidney Gilchrist Thomas, Percy Carlyle Gilchrist and the basic Bessemer Process').
7. Hendrick, *Life of Andrew Carnegie*, p. 314; *The Chester Courant and Advertiser for North Wales*, 15 October 1902, reported the opening.
8. For the popularity of eisteddfodau in the mining towns of Pennsylvania, see, for example, W. D. Jones, *Wales in America; Scranton and the Welsh, 1860–1920* (Cardiff, 1993), pp. 97–105; and Gage, *American Prometheus*, pp. 127–8, records both men's support for the Pittsburgh eisteddfod.
9. *The Cambrian News and Merionethshire Standard*, 2 May 1902.

10. *The Carnarvon and Denbigh Herald and North and South Wales Independent,* 8 June 1906; *The North Wales Express,* 20 July 1906; *Cardiff Times,* 25 August 1906. For Lloyd George and the eisteddfodau of 1902 and 1906, see E. Price, *Lloyd George a'r eisteddfod genedlaethol a phrifwyliau Bangor a Chaernarfon* (Caernarfon, 2005), chs 3 and 4 (pp. 28–47). The closeness of the relationship between the two men during the First World War is suggested by the £2,000 legacy which Carnegie left to Lloyd George in his will: P. Rowland, *Lloyd George* (London, 1975), pp. 514, 593.

11. Gwent Archives, D385/1, pp. 227, 234, 248. On 29 September 1903, Rogerstone parish council resolved to thank Carnegie for his promise of £1,400 for a new library building.

12. National Library of Wales, William George (Solicitor) Papers, 1401: letter to William George from David Lloyd George, House of Commons, 6 May 1904.

13. W. A. Munford, *A History of the Library Association, 1877–1977* (London, 1976), pp. 78, 334, 339; see text p. 47. See J. Piggott, 'Clive, Robert George Windsor, Baron Windsor and earl of Plymouth', in *ODNB, s.n.* For Windsor's persistence on behalf of public libraries in the house of commons during 1898–1901, see R. J. B. Morris, *Parliament and the Public Libraries* (London, 1977), pp. 99–106.

14. Munford, *History of the Library Association,* pp. 79, 141, 155–6, 334; see text. p. 44. For John Herbert Lewis, see *DWB,* p. 556.

6. CREATING CARNEGIE LIBRARIES

1. For details of Bertram's life and work for Carnegie, see F. P. Hill, *James Bertram: An Appreciation* (New York, 1936), esp. pp. 15–22 (the early years) and pp. 38–65 (on grants for libraries and organs). Frank Hill was Brooklyn librarian and knew Bertram well.

2. For this schedule, see Nasaw, *Andrew Carnegie,* pp. 605–7.

3. For the 'Notes', see Hill, *James Bertram,* pp. 44–7.

4. For Colwyn Bay's clock tower, see *The Welsh Coast Pioneer and Review for North Cambria,* 4 December 1903, which includes Bertram's letter of 21 November from New York. The tower was never built.

5. *Weekly Mail,* 19 July 1902; *The Welsh Coast Pioneer and Review for North Cambria,* 11 December 1903; *Llandudno Advertiser and List of Visitors,* 21 October 1905.

6. *The Evening Express,* 16 June 1905; Glamorgan Archives, BB/C/3/39, p. 24 (11 January 1904); Glamorgan Archives, BB/C/3/40, pp. 10, 18, 23 (for the quotation, 5 September 1904), p. 34 (the award of the arbitration, 6 February 1905). Carnegie had earlier refused a request from Barry to increase his original grant by £2,000 to build two other reading rooms; he commented that £8,000

was perfectly appropriate for Barry's proposed new library and its income from the rates: *Barry Herald*, 28 August 1903; Glamorgan Archives, BB/C/3/39, pp. 10, 15 (James Bertram's reply, 28 August 1903).

7.   O. Prizeman, *Philanthropy and Light: Carnegie Libraries and the Advent of Transatlantic Standards for Public Space* (Farnham, 2012), p. 171. A number of plans for Welsh libraries have survived, the results sometimes of Bertram's comments, sometimes of arguments within library committees: see, for example, Glamorgan Archives, BC/5/1/16234 (Canton library plan, 1906); Flintshire Archives, D-DM/1109/1–9, 11, 16–27 (Rhyl library, 1904–); Powys Archives, R/X 137/10 and RC/A/1/309 (Llandrindod Wells library, 1911); Conwy Archives, CMostyn Estate Plans, 7 and 8 (Llandudno library, 1908).

8.   *The Evening Express*, 9 March 1904. For John Lloyd, see *DWB*, p. 584.

9.   For the influence of Andrew Carnegie's library building programme on library design and specialization within the architectural profession, see J. W. P. Campbell, *The Library: A World History* (London, 2013), pp. 2, 236, 506.

10. Thompson, *Library Buildings of Britain and Europe*, p. 15; see text. p. 60. The important study, Prizeman, *Philanthropy and Light*, pp. xxi, 2, 7, 10, 28, 50, and ch. 2 ('Setting standards for public light'), provides a valuable context for study of the Welsh libraries. On individual designated rooms, Prizeman, *Philanthropy and Light*, pp. 178–9, 187–8; and the quotation, p. 205.

11. Prizeman, *Philanthropy and Light*, p. 110; Ceredigion Archives, ABM/SE/1/6, pp. 37, 147–8, 151–2, 439–40, 446–7.

12. The final bill was paid to Henry Smith by B. J. Francis on 7 September 1906. Gwent Archives, Abergavenny Library Papers, D1348/11, p. 9.

7.   BUILDING THE CARNEGIE LIBRARIES OF WALES

1.   For the siting of Carnegie libraries in Great Britain, see Prizeman, *Philanthropy and Light*, pp. xxii, 82, 128–9.

2.   *The Cambrian*, 11 August 1902.

3.   Denbighshire Archives, DD/G/2207047, an acknowledgement of receipt of the book by James K. Hardie at the Skibo estate office, 4 March 1901; the book may have been J. Randall, *Our Coal and Iron Industries, and the Men who have Wrought in Connection with them: The Wilkinsons* (Madeley, 1879). See also DD/G/2207041, 7 March 1901, a further letter from Edward Hughes, who eagerly sent Carnegie a recent cutting from the *Manchester Guardian* about Wrexham's connection with 'the Iron and Engineering trades' which he felt sure would be of interest to Carnegie; and DD/G/2207043, 26 July 1901, Hardie's reply to another letter, sent

by Hughes two days earlier, assuring him that his communications will have been placed before Carnegie 'along with many others'.

4. A. Carnegie, *James Watt* (London and New York, 1905).

5. National Records of Scotland, GD281/3/54 and GD281/3/88, record the correspondence with these two local authorities.

6. Gwent Archives, A320/M/7, p. 182.

7. *The Welsh Coast Pioneer and Review for North Cambria*, 11 July 1902, 15 August 1902; *Cheshire Observer*, 22 August 1903. The library at Flint was opened by Lewis in August 1903 with space for 2,000 volumes.

8. *The Welsh Coast Pioneer and Review for North Cambria*, 4 September 1903; *Prestatyn Weekly*, 14 January 1905; *Rhyl Journal*, 25 March 1905 (recording the 'consternation') and 27 January 1906.

9. A. H. Dodd, *A History of Wrexham, Denbighshire* (Wrexham, 1957), pp. 120, 130–1; *Cheshire Observer*, 30 January 1904.

10. Ceredigion Archives, ABM/SE/1/5, pp. 664–5, 671–2, 674–5, 675, 691. The district council finally agreed to buy the entire site on 12 January 1904 (p. 703).

11. *Cheshire Observer*, 5 July 1902.

12. *Llandudno Advertiser and List of Visitors*, 24 August 1907.

13. *Carnarvon and Denbigh Herald and North and South Wales Independent*, 23 May 1908, 16 September 1910.

14. *Cambrian News*, 25 April 1905.

15. See J.V. Hughes, 'The history of libraries in the Port Talbot district', *Transactions of the Port Talbot History Society*, 4/2 (2000), 108–37 (especially 127–31); *The Cambrian*, 11 July 1902; *The Cambria Daily Leader*, 20 July 1914. Miss Talbot also gave £100 for the purchase of books for the library.

16. West Glamorgan Archives, D/D T958.

17. *Evening Express*, 1 and 11 March 1905.

18. *County Observer and Monmouthshire Central Advertiser*, 12 March 1904; *Evening Express*, 6 November 1905; Gwent Archives D385/1, pp. 227, 234, 241, 243. Lord Tredegar was reported to be much in favour of the scheme and had agreed to offer the site by March 1904: Gwent Archives D385/1, pp. 248–9, 264. See *https://www.imeche.org* for a biography of Edward Windsor Richards.

19. *Evening Express*, 1 July 1903, 19 October 1905, 31 July 1907. The deed conveying the site of both library and institute to the council was handed over in April 1907, prior to the duke's visit: Gwent Archives A320/M/8, p. 358. His agent arranged for the transfer of 2,000 books from All Souls College, Oxford, in October 1908: *Cardiff Times*, 24 October 1908.

20. Gwent Archives, A433/M/12, pp. 4, 21, 126, 274. Discussions with Hanbury began in July 1905, and on 21 October the clerk of the council reported that the proposed site was 'beyond our anticipation': Gwent Archives,

A433/M/12, pp. 370, 398; Gwent Archives, A433/M/14–15; Gwent Archives, D454/1403 (correspondence with the copyhold owners); *Weekly Mail*, 23 December 1905.

21. Gwent Archives, A433/M/13, pp. 139, 153, 174, 205. For John Capel Hanbury's other gifts of land in Pontypool, for a hospital and West Monmouthshire School, see R. Hanbury-Tennison, *The Hanburys of Monmouthshire* (privately printed, Aberystwyth, 1995), pp. 330, 342.

22. *Weekly Mail*, 26 September 1903; *The Public Library Journal*, 4/4 (September 1903), 14–15, which carries James Bertram's letter, 4 July 1903, granting £4,000 to Penarth provided a site was made available and the maximum rate assessment of £372 per annum was levied, as the local council had originally stated.

23. *Merthyr Express*, 28 June 1902; *County Observer and Monmouthshire Central Advertiser*, 28 June 1902; *The North Wales Express*, 27 June 1902, also reported this ambitious scheme. By July 1905 Carnegie had increased the amount to £12,300: see A. Bowen, *History of the Libraries in the Borough of Merthyr Tydfil and District, 1846–1946* (Merthyr Tydfil, n.d.), pp. 17–27, and A. Donaldson and I. Macleod, 'Andrew Carnegie: The injustice of ranks and the crisis of wealth', *Merthyr Historian*, 14 (2002), 167–86 (especially 167). For David Alfred Thomas, later Viscount Rhondda (1856–1918), see *DWB*, pp. 942–3.

24. *Weekly Mail*, 10 January 1903.

25. *Cardiff Times*, 14 March 1908; *Evening Express*, 20 October 1909.

26. *Evening Express*, 4 June 1902.

27. *Cardiff Times*, 28 June 1902, 7 March and 16 November 1935.

28. Glamorgan Archives, BCOW/C/96/24, a draft letter addressed to Andrew Carnegie at Skibo castle, November 1903, from the chairman and secretary of Cowbridge's borough council.

29. *The Pembrokeshire Herald and General Advertiser*, 13 February 1903, 30 November 1906; *The Pembrokeshire County Guardian and Cardigan Reporter*, 25 June 1903, 30 November 1906. Henry Owen's manuscripts and most of his books were eventually deposited at the new National Library of Wales in Aberystwyth.

30. Compare the regional variations in architectural styles of Ireland's Carnegie libraries, in Grimes, *Irish Carnegie Libraries*, ch. 9 (pp. 60–71).

31. *Llandudno Advertiser and List of Visitors*, 6 May 1905; Dodd, *A History of Wrexham, Denbighshire*, pp. 120, 130–1. Hodge's bid to be the architect of Bangor's library a year or so later was unsuccessful.

32. Gwent Archives, A433/M/12, pp. 414–15; Gwent Archives, A433/M/13, pp. 11, 38–9, 323–4.

33. *The Evening Express*, 20 October 1909.

34. *Cardiff Times*, 15 November 1902; *Barry Dock News*, 19 December 1902; *Barry Herald*, 9 October 1903. The architects had produced working drawings for the new library by 1 May 1903: Glamorgan Archives, BB/C/3/39, pp. 6–7, 11.

35. For Canton's plans, see RCAHMW, Welsh School of Architecture Collection, D5/47, H3/11 (NA/GEN/97/044e). On E. M. Bruce Vaughan's buildings from the 1880s, see J. Newman, *The Buildings of Wales: Glamorgan* (London, 1995), pp. 95–6, 104, 109–11, 301, and T. Lloyd, J. Orbach and R. Scourfield, *The Buildings of Wales: Carmarthenshire and Ceredigion* (New Haven and London, 2006), pp. 44–5. For Vaughan himself (1856–1919), see *DWB*, https://www.biography.wales/.

36. *Evening Express*, 28 February 1905, 7 July 1905. The council had agreed to donate the two sites by March 1904: *Weekly Mail*, 12 March 1904.

37. *Carnarvon and Denbigh Herald and North and South Wales Independent*, 23 May 1908.

38. *Llandudno Advertiser and List of Visitors*, 29 April 1905, which also notes that the contractors were local too, Messrs Robert Evans and Sons of Old Colwyn. For J. M. Porter, see E. Hubbard, *The Buildings of Wales: Clwyd* (London, 1986), pp. 84, 134, 138.

39. *The Cambria Daily Leader*, 16 July 1914, announcing the laying of Tai-bach library's foundation stone. The contractor for this work was J. Vaughan John of Port Talbot.

40. *Carnarvon and Denbigh Herald and North and South Wales Independent*, 7 April 1905 and 28 September 1906; *Cardiff Times*, 1 September 1906.

41. RCAHMW, NGR58/30/81/81 (from Cadw's official listing), and with images of the tiles in RCAHMW, C86011, a photograph of a tile taken c.1984.

42. It is said that on one side the cartouche has the remains of a bearded face: could this be of Andrew Carnegie himself, as at Abergavenny? See text. p. 55.

43. See RCAHMW, Cadw listing NJR 29/07/2008.

44. RCAHMW, 31822, from Cadw listing no. 13404.

45. RCAHMW, 31948; Gwent Archives, Abergavenny Library Papers, D1348/6 (a report from the architect to the library committee).

46. See *The Criccieth Heritage Walk*, 2nd edn (Cricieth, 2003), brought to my attention by Dr John Law.

47. Wall, *Andrew Carnegie*, p. 819; Mackay, *Little Boss*, pp. 255–7.

48. The identification of the figure with the Virgin Mary must be mistaken.

49. RCAHMW, 31822, from Cadw listing no. 13404.

50. Ceredigion Archives, ABM/SE/1/6, pp. 661, 701; Gwent Archives, Newport Borough Council, A110/A/M/14, pp. 134, 330–1.

51. For a photograph of Carnegie in front of Abergavenny's new library on the occasion of his award of the freedom, see Gwent Archives, D1348/13, misdated to the opening of the library the previous year.

52. Ceredigion Archives, ABM/SE/1/6, pp. 37, 147–8, 151–2, 169–70, 197.

53. Gwent Archives, D1348/8, the architect's plan of 1903; Gwent Archives, D1348/5, Bertram's letter from Skibo castle in Scotland, 18 July 1904.

54. *County Observer and Monmouthshire Central Advertiser*, 8 April 1905.

55. Dodd, *A History of Wrexham, Denbighshire*, p. 120; *Cambrian News*, 25 April 1905.

56. D. Sellwood, 'The libraries that never were', *The Journal of the Caerphilly Local History Society*, 8 (2007), 28–35 (at 25, quoting Cardiff City Libraries Committee, *Annual Report*, 1907). For Tai-bach's 'juvenile library', 'reference and magazine room', lending library, ladies' reading room, librarian's office and, upstairs, a large lecture hall, and the furnishings and fittings, see West Glamorgan Archives, NPT/42 (1915).

57. Gwent Archives, D1348, with the poster displayed in Abergavenny Museum (1915).

58. Ceredigion Archives, ABM SE/1/6, p. 508; *Wrexham Advertiser*, 1 October 1904. Original Edwardian chairs, tables, a newspaper rack and other furniture from Canton's Carnegie library were donated to the National History Museum at St Fagans (accession no. F91.30) in 1991, a reference I owe to Dr Sioned Williams. They are now on display, ironically, in the reconstructed Oakdale Workmen's Institute.

59. Denbighshire Archives, PCD/6/136, vol. relating to Bersham Parish Council, Carnegie Free Library, 1905–30; *The Wrexham Advertiser*, 1 October 1904; see also 'The Centenary of Coedpoeth Library', compiled by D. Hughes and P. Jeorrett for Coedpoeth Community Council.

60. *Carnarvon and Denbigh Herald and North and South Wales Independent*, 9 August 1907. The offer came from the Smithsonian itself and may have been prompted by the fact that David Lloyd George was a member of the British cabinet at this juncture. He and his wife were due to visit Skibo castle in September 1908: *Cambrian News and Merionethshire Standard*, 21 August 1908.

61. *Aberdare Leader*, 23 May 1903.

62. *Wrexham Advertiser*, 12 December 1904. For A. N. Palmer, see *DWB*, pp. 727–8. Compare the similarly catholic collection of books listed in other printed Carnegie library catalogues, see text p. 64.

63. *North Wales Gazette*, February 1905; *Cambrian News*, 25 April 1905 (for the quotation). 'Reasonable and rational social intercourse and recreation' evidently included the library's billiard team, which, however, lost to Pwllheli Liberal Club in March 1914: *North Wales Chronicle*, 20 March 1914.

64. Glamorgan Archives, P6/62, pp. 116–17.

65. *Evening Express*, 11 June 1907.

66. West Glamorgan Archives, D/D T958. Sir Samuel had married his second wife quite recently, in 1905.

67. *The Cambrian*, 16 June 1905.
68. Gwent Archives, A110/A/M/14, p. 444; *Evening Express*, 15 March 1907.
69. Gwent Archives, D1348/14, pp. 18, 20, 22.
70. Flintshire Archives, D-L/D/1/9; Denbighshire Archives, DD/W/129; Glamorgan Archives, DXDQ: Abercanaid library printed catalogue, 1909, 6pp. For Rhyl's new catalogues of its lending and reference departments, 1908, see National Library of Wales, XZ921.
71. Ceredigion Archives, ABM/SE/1/6, pp. 661, 701, including James Bertram's letter of 21 December 1905 on Carnegie's behalf.
72. See *Cambrian News and Merionethshire Standard*, 27 April 1906, on the opening.
73. *Wrexham Advertiser*, 10 December 1904.
74. *The Weekly News and Visitors' Chronicle for Colwyn Bay*, 28 April 1905.
75. *Rhyl Record and Advertiser*, 6 April 1907; Flintshire Record Office, D-DM/1109/D/5, a photograph of the event. In August 1903, Lewis had also opened the Carnegie library within Flint's town hall, on the ground floor, financed with a £200 grant which the MP had evidently secured from Andrew Carnegie: *The Welsh Coast Pioneer and Review for North Cambria*, 15 August 1902.
76. *Weekly Mail*, 30 August 1902; *Evening Express*, 11 March 1903.
77. *Cardiff Times*, 20 September 1902; *Evening Express*, 15 April 1907, with the gift reported on 11 June 1907.
78. *Evening Express*, 21 June; *County Observer and Monmouthshire Central Advertiser*, 28 June 1902; Bowen, *The History of the Libraries in the Borough of Merthyr Tydfil and District, 1846–1946*, pp. 17–27. For the compliment, see text p. 49.
79. *The Cardiff Times*, 1 September 1906.
80. *The Chester Courant and Advertiser for North Wales*, 20 February 1907. Denbighshire Archives, DD/G/2207044-5, is the programme for the opening of Wrexham's library which took place during the mayoralty of Alderman Edward Hughes who may first have broached the possibility of a Carnegie grant in 1901 (see above). Sir Foster Cunliffe (1875–1916), a fellow of All Souls College, Oxford, died at the battle of the Somme in 1916.
81. *Carnarvon and Denbigh Herald and North and South Wales Independent*, 16 September 1910.
82. *The Cardiff Times*, 2 September 1905.
83. *Glamorgan Gazette*, 30 August 1907.
84. *Weekly Mail*, 9 March 1907. John Ballinger (1860–1933) had been Cardiff's librarian since 1884 and would soon be the first librarian of the National Library of Wales: *DWB*, pp. 23–4.

8. ABORTIVE PROPOSALS FOR CARNEGIE LIBRARIES

1. *Cardiff Times*, 26 September 1903.
2. Gwent Archives, Newport Borough Council, A110/A/M/13, pp. 61, 134, 332, 385; Gwent Archives, Newport Borough Council, A110/A/M /14, pp. 444, 331.
3. *The Cambrian*, 31 October 1902, 3 April 1903, 8 March 1904 and 23 December 1904, charts the laborious discussions to a conclusion. Carnegie had formally offered £8,000 on 22 October 1903, having had an opportunity to scrutinize the plans and elevations for the proposed buildings.
4. West Glamorgan Archives, SL Lib. 5/2, the scheme as approved and printed, 1904. In other wards, tenancy agreements were still made by the town council for other branch libraries to continue in rented accommodation: West Glamorgan Archives, SL Lib. 5/3.
5. *The Cambrian*, 10 June 1904; National Records of Scotland, GD281/3/309 (20 February 1905).
6. *Evening Express*, 10 July 1902. For Tredegar's workmen's library, see Roe, 'The Public Library in Wales', 200. Lord Tredegar had already gifted Bedwellty park and house to the town to serve as a council house in April 1901, and eventually the Temperance Hall itself was transferred to the workmen's institute: see D. J. Davies, *Ninety Years of Endeavour: The Tredegar Workmen's Hall, 1861–1951* (Cardiff, 1951), pp. 48–59, though this does not mention the possibility of approaching Andrew Carnegie.
7. *Evening Express*, 11 November 1903.
8. *Evening Express*, 6 February 1903.
9. *Evening Express*, 14 March 1903.
10. *Evening Express*, 28 February 1903 (for the opening of negotiations) and 3 December 1904; *Weekly Mail*, 23 December 1905. The library was opened in September 1908: *The Cardiff Times*, 26 September 1908.
11. *Evening Express*, 27 March 1905; *Caerphilly Journal*, 22 March 1906 (for the quotation). 'The Library Question' is fully discussed in Sellwood, 'The libraries that never were', *The Journal of the Caerphilly Local History Society*, 8 (1907), 28–35, which also relies on Glamorgan Archives, Caerphilly urban district council minutes.
12. In general, see Mackay, *Little Boss*, pp. 255–7.
13. *The Chester Courant and Advertiser for North Wales*, 5 August 1903 (for Connah's Quay). See, in general, Jones, 'Public Libraries in Wales since 1862', 216–17.
14. *The Cambrian News and Merionethshire Standard*, 14 November 1902; *Welsh Gazette and West Wales Advertiser*, 15 January 1903.
15. *Aberdare Leader*, 4 October 1902, 9 July 1904 and 10 November 1906.
16. *Aberdare Leader*, 4 October 1902.

17. C. M. Baggs, 'The miners' libraries of South Wales from the 1860s to 1939' (unpublished PhD thesis, Aberystwyth University, 2 vols, 1995), vol. 1, 112–16 (commenting on relations between Carnegie and institute libraries) and 224–34 (on a wider membership).

18. C. M. Baggs, '"Carnegie offered money and a lot of South Wales refused to have it: it was blood money": Bringing public libraries to the South Wales valleys, 1870 to 1939', *Library History*, 17 (November 2001), 171. For a list of miners' libraries in Glamorgan and Monmouthshire from 1865 to the First World War, see Roe, 'The Public Library in Wales', 200.

19. *Evening Express*, 2 September 1902; *Weekly Mail*, 6 September 1902.

20. *The Cambrian*, 12 September 1902.

21. *The Cambrian*, 17 October 1902.

22. *Evening Express*, 9 March 1904; Roe, 'The Public Library in Wales', 84.

9. THE CARNEGIE LEGACY IN WALES

1. Wall, *Andrew Carnegie*, pp. 836–7. For Lord Rendel's eight-page appeal in January 1901, followed by a further letter to Carnegie in the following November, see National Library of Wales, Aberystwyth Old Students' Association, UNC/1 (a printed copy of the appeal), and NLW MS 19440E, ff. 52–3, 56a, 56b, with comment in E. L. Ellis, *The University College of Wales, Aberystwyth, 1872–1972* (Cardiff, 1972), pp. 132–3.

2. P. Stead, *Coleg Harlech: The First Fifty Years* (Cardiff, 1977), pp. 28–9.

3. Goodenough, *The Greatest Good Fortune*, pp. 259–60; Nasaw, *Andrew Carnegie*, pp. 607–8.

4. *Llandudno Advertiser and List of Visitors*, 1 October 1904; *Carnarvon and Denbigh Herald and North and South Wales Independent*, 5 October 1906; *Evening Express*, 1 December 1906.

5. *The County Echo*, 28 September 1905; *Carnarvon and Denbigh Herald and North and South Wales Independent*, 3 August 1906.

6. H. Edwards, *Capel Llanelli: Our Rich Heritage* (Carmarthen, 2009), pp. 447–8.

7. *The North Wales Express*, 8 February 1907; *Carnarvon and Denbigh Herald and North and South Wales Independent*, 15 October 1909; *Welsh Gazette and West Wales Advertiser*, 11 October 1906.

8. *Merthyr Express*, 19 March 1910; *Abergavenny Chronicle*, 15 April 1910.

9. Klein, *Change Makers*, pp. 1–17; Tweedale, 'Andrew Carnegie (1835–1919)', in *ODNB, s.n.* The endowment for the Peace Palace was inaugurated as early as 1903. Carnegie's various philanthropic projects between 1879 and 1914 are helpfully listed, with the amounts invested in them, in Harvey, Maclean,

Gordon and Shaw, 'Andrew Carnegie and the foundations of contemporary entrepreneurial philanthropy', 427.

10. 'William George Stewart Adams (1874–1966)', by B. Harrison, *ODNB, s.n.*

11. See E. C. Lagemann, *The Politics of Knowledge: The Carnegie Corporation, Philanthropy and Public Policy* (Chicago, 1992), pp. 6–24, on the early days of the Corporation before Carnegie's death in 1919.

12. *The Brecon Radnor Express, Carmarthen and Swansea Valley Gazette and Brynmawr District Advertiser*, 1 January 1914; Hill, *James Bertram*, pp. 34–7.

13. Roe, 'The Public Library in Wales', 75–109 (with the first county libraries, 75–9); T. E. Griffiths, 'Caernarvonshire and its libraries: development of the first county library in Wales', *Transactions of the Caernarvonshire Historical Society*, 33 (1972), 170–89 (especially 171–4). Photographs of Margaret Carnegie Miller's visit to Aberystwyth library are held by Ceredigion Archives.

14. Baggs, 'Carnegie offered money and a lot of South Wales refused to have it', 176; D. S. Scott, *Public Library Development in Glamorgan, 1920 to 1974: An Area Study with particular reference to Glamorgan County Library* (Library Association, 1979); Jones, 'Public libraries in Wales since 1862', 220. Indeed, Mountain Ash's resistance lasted until 1963.

GAZETTEER OF CARNEGIE LIBRARIES BUILT IN WALES

The libraries are listed in alphabetical order and located by their pre-1974 counties.

ABERCANAID BRANCH LIBRARY, GLAMORGAN

Location: on Alexander Place; the site was purchased by Merthyr urban district council from the owners of the Wingfield and Mackintosh estate at little over £100.
Carnegie grant: £700 in 1902.
Architect: T. F. Harvey, surveyor of Merthyr Tydfil urban district council.
Contractor: Enoch Williams of Dowlais.
The branch library and reading room was opened in January 1903.
Description: a small, single-storey building similar to the Carnegie libraries at Aberfan and Troedyrhiw.
Present use: demolished.

ABERFAN BRANCH LIBRARY, GLAMORGAN

Location: on the corner of Bridge Street and Riverside Close.
Carnegie grant: £700 in 1902.
The branch library and reading room was opened in January 1903.
Description: a small one-storey building with tall neo-Gothic windows.
Present use: recently modernized, it is used as a meeting hall for community groups.

ABERGAVENNY, MONMOUTHSHIRE
National Records of Scotland, GD281/3/2, 9 July 1902–18 September 1905.
Location: on Baker Street opposite Holy Trinity Church; the site was purchased by the town council in 1904 from Miss Rachel Herbert's charity with the agreement of Holy Trinity Church Trust.
Carnegie grant: £2,000 in 1902.
Architect: B. J. Francis.
Contractor: H. Smith of Kidderminster.
The foundation stone was laid on 6 April 1905 by the mayor of Abergavenny, Major W. Williams, chairman of the library committee.
The library was opened on 8 September 1906 by the marquess of Abergavenny and the Lord Mayor of London, Sir Walter Vaughan Morgan of Breconshire.
Description: a Grade II listed building (Cadw 2886), in the late neo-Gothic style, of rock-faced sandstone with Bath stone dressings. It has two large reading rooms set at oblique angles to each other and linked by a stepped entrance wing, one reading room, hexagonal, to the left and the lending library to the right, oblong in shape. It had provision for 6,500 volumes, with a museum on the floor above.
Present use: as Abergavenny's town library.
In June 1907 Andrew Carnegie was made a freeman of Abergavenny.

ABERYSTWYTH, CARDIGANSHIRE
National Records of Scotland, GD281/3/3 file, 26 February 1903–22 September 1908.
Location: on Corporation Street facing Albert Square, where it is set into a row of street frontages; the site was provided by Aberystwyth borough council.
Carnegie Grant: £3,000 in 1903; the rateable assessment was £170 per annum.
Architect: Walter G. Payton of Birmingham.
Contractor: Messrs Edwards Bros of Trefechan.
The foundation stone was laid on 28 July 1905 by David Davies of Llandinam.
The library was opened in April 1906 by Mrs Vaughan Davies of Tanybwlch, the wife of Cardiganshire's Liberal MP, Matthew Lewis Vaughan Davies.
Description: a Grade II listed building (Cadw 10209). An Edwardian Classical building in seventeenth-century style, of two storeys, with brown rubble stone frontage and red sandstone banding and dressings. The chimney stacks are of red brick, and there is art nouveau lettering over the panelled

doorway. It has a fine interior, with art nouveau green-glazed foliage ornament beside the staircases. The library had space for 14,000 books (RCAHMW, NPRN 23277; NGR 58/30/81/81 (Cadw listing 24 November 1987), including external photograph).
Present use: neglected.

BANGOR, CAERNARFONSHIRE
National Records of Scotland, GD281/3/23 file, 19 August 1903–23 November 1949.
Location: between the cathedral canonry and the proposed new post office; the site was provided by Bangor city corporation.
Carnegie grant: £2,500 in 1903, supplemented by £500 from Captain John Jones's legacy.
Architect: A. E. Dixon and C. H. Potter of Manchester.
Contractor: Messrs Hughes and Stirling of Liverpool.
The library was opened on 8 November 1907 by Lord Penrhyn.
Description: a Grade II listed building (Cadw 3979). A single-storey building in Edwardian Baroque style with Ruabon brick frontage and ashlar dressings. The octagonal inner porch is lit by a central dome.
Present use: as Bangor's city library.

BARRY, GLAMORGAN
National Records of Scotland, GD281/3/25 file, October 1901–9 March 1906.
Location: on King's Square, on the site of Maes-y-cwm quarry, which was provided by the town council.
Carnegie grant: £8,000 in 1902 and a further £500 in 1905.
Architect: Charles E. Hutchinson and E. Harding Payne of London.
Contractor: Watkin Williams of Cardiff.
The library was opened on St David's Day 1906 by the earl of Plymouth.
Description: a Grade II listed building (Cadw 13404). A two-storey building, with an attic, in Edwardian Baroque style, of red brick with Bath stone dressings and large Ionic columns. There is a clock tower at the junction with the contemporary town hall. On each side of steps up to the entrance is a seated stone lion with a cartouche between its front paws. The library had space for 30,000 volumes, with 4,500 for the reference library, and seating for 115 readers.
Present use: as Barry's town library.
For an account of the library, see Awbery, *Let Us Talk of Barry,* and Moore (ed.), *Barry: The Centenary Book.*

BRIDGEND, GLAMORGAN

National Records of Scotland, GD281/3/48 file, 24 October 1901–20 January 1926.

Location: on Wyndham Street; Lord Dunraven defrayed three-quarters of the cost of the site owned by the town hall trustees, with £150 raised by subscription.

Carnegie grant: £2,000 in 1902.

Architect: P. J. Thomas of Bridgend.

Contractor: Messrs Price and Morgan of Bridgend.

The library was opened on 29 August 1907 by John Randall, the agent of the Dunraven estate.

Description: a Grade II listed building (Cadw 11308). A narrow Baroque frontage with Bath stone dressings and a domed entrance hall.

Present use: as a community facility and now proudly named Carnegie House Arts Centre.

BRYNMAWR, MONMOUTHSHIRE

National Records of Scotland, GD281/3/53 file, 21 July 1902–16 October 1933.

Location: on Market Square; the site was presented by the duke of Beaufort.

Carnegie grant: £1,250 in 1903.

Architect: E. K. Bates of Newport.

Contractor: John Jenkins of Brynmawr.

The library was opened in October 1905 by Llewelyn Thomas JP. The adjoining Brynmawr institute was completed the following year.

Description: built with local stone and Ebbw Vale brick with blue Pennant stone dressings, it has two large rooms on two storeys, the main reading room on the ground floor with storage for 6,000 volumes. The entrance doorway was carved in Forest of Dean stone.

Present use: as Brynmawr and District Museum.

BUCKLEY, FLINTSHIRE

National Records of Scotland, GD281/3/54 file, 20 September 1901–17 September 1907.

Location: adjacent to the town hall on Mold Road; the site was offered by Thomas and Robert Griffiths of Chester.

Carnegie grant: £1,600 offered in 1902. H. H. Phipps, one of the principal partners in the Carnegie Steel Trust, offered a supplementary gift of £25.

Architect: R. Cecil Davies.

The town hall was begun in 1901 and the adjoining library the following year. The library was opened on 7 September 1904.

Description: a Grade II listed building (Cadw 87599) along with the town council offices. The building is in local red brick with stone dressings, in a domestic style with Arts and Crafts influences.

Present use: since 1977 it has been part of the council offices and is now used for small business units.

CANTON BRANCH LIBRARY, CARDIFF. GLAMORGAN

National Records of Scotland, GD281/3/61 file, 5 July 1902–10 July 1911.

Location: at the corner of Library Road and Cowbridge Road East; the site was provided by Cardiff's town council.

Carnegie grant: £5,000 in 1902.

Architect: R. M. Bruce Vaughan of Cardiff.

The library was opened by the Lord Mayor of Cardiff on 7 March 1907, in the presence of Hew Morrison, Andrew Carnegie's designated representative.

Description: a Grade II listed building (Cadw 25856). In the style of a Flemish late-medieval building, it is of grey-brown sandstone rubble with Bath stone dressings and a Welsh slate roof. Internally, it had two large reading rooms and a separate children's room.

Present use: as Canton branch library.

CATHAYS BRANCH LIBRARY, CARDIFF. GLAMORGAN

National Records of Scotland, GD281/3/61 file, 5 July 1902–10 July 1911.

Location: on a site between Whitchurch Road and Fairoak Road.

Carnegie grant: £5,000 in 1902.

Architect: Speir and Beavan of Cardiff.

Contractor: W. T. Morgan of Cardiff, with sculpture by T. A. Jones of Cardiff and stained glass by Harvey and Arshby of Birmingham.

The library was opened on 7 March 1907 by the Lord Mayor of Cardiff and Hew Morrison, Andrew Carnegie's designated representative.

Description: the only Grade II* listed building among Wales's Carnegie libraries (Cadw 13681). Its unusual butterfly plan of a single storey echoes Arts and Crafts designs elsewhere in England. It is built of rock-faced stone with Bath stone dressings and a slate roof. A single spire rises from a narrow central octagonal tower. On either side of the central lending area are outer wings which housed the children's and the adults' reading rooms, with an adjacent ladies' reading room. There is art nouveau glass as decoration.

Present use: as Cathays branch library.

CHURCH VILLAGE (OR LLANTWIT FARDRE), GLAMORGAN

National Records of Scotland, GD281/3/203 file, 10 March 1904–11 January 1965.

Location: on Main Road.

Carnegie grant: £1,500.

Architect: Arthur Ll. Thomas of Pontypridd.

Contractor: Messrs Price Bros of Cardiff.

The library was opened on 2 September 1906 by Sir D. Alfred Thomas MP in the presence of the parish councillors and the Revd John Jenkins.

Description: a Grade II listed building (Cadw 23523). In a free Renaissance style in grey stone with prominent concrete dressings painted white. The two-storey building incorporates some art nouveau stained glass depicting vines. Internally there is an open barrelled roof space. The library had space for 3,000 volumes and 20 newspapers.

Present use: as a community and parish hall.

COEDPOETH (OR BERSHAM), DENBIGHSHIRE

National Records of Scotland, GD 281/3/30 file (Bersham), 5 May 1903–6 October 1969.

Location: on Park Road, Coedpoeth.

Carnegie grant: £1,500 in 1904.

Architect: William Moss.

Contractor: Samuel Moss.

The library was opened on 12 December 1904 by Samuel Moss MP.

Description: a two-storey rectangular building in heavy local stone, with decorated ceilings internally. On the ground floor were a large games room, a refreshment room and council room where the parish council and other bodies might meet; on the first floor were two large rooms, a parish room and a reading room, a combined parish hall and library, with reference and lending areas.

See the account of the library by D. Hughes and P. Jeorrett for Coedpoeth Community Council; see also Denbighshire Archives, PCD/6/136: Bersham Parish Council Carnegie Free Library, 1905–30.

Present use: as a community centre.

COLWYN BAY, DENBIGHSHIRE

National Records of Scotland, GD281/3/83 file, 21 June 1902–25 June 1912.

Location: on Woodland Road West; the site was provided by the new town, assisted by public subscription.

Carnegie grant: in 1902 Andrew Carnegie agreed to provide £1,000 and to match a sum raised by public subscription, up to £1,500; in December 1903 he raised his grant to £3,000.

Architect: Messrs Porter and Hunter of Chadwick and Booth of Manchester and Colwyn Bay.

Contractor: Messrs Robert Evans and Sons of Old Colwyn.

The foundation stone was laid in 1902.

The library, which was built to commemorate the coronation of Edward VII in 1902, was opened in April 1905 by J. Herbert Roberts MP and was known as the Coronation Free Library.

Description: an imposing red brick building of two storeys.

Present use: as the Colwyn Bay library.

CRICIETH, CAERNARFONSHIRE

National Records of Scotland, GD281/3/88 file, 27 October 1901–16 February 1905.

Location: on the High Street; a site offered by J. T. Jones of Parciau, chairman of the urban district council.

Carnegie grant: £800 in 1902, with a further £100 gifted by the lord lieutenant of Caernarfonshire, J. E. Greaves.

Architect: Rowland Lloyd Jones, the county architect.

Contractor: David Evans of Cricieth.

The library was opened on St David's Day 1905 by J. E. Greaves, lord lieutenant of Caernarfonshire.

Description: The building is in domestic style of red Ruabon brick with Talacre stone dressings; its upper part is roughcast with red brick dressing. Some windows and the inner door have art nouveau decoration. The reading room and lending library were on the ground floor, with bookcases for 6,000 volumes and space for a further 3,000.

Present use: as a community facility, since 2017.

DEINIOLEN, CAERNARFONSHIRE

National Records of Scotland, GD281/3/200 file (as Llanddeiniolen), 10 March 1909–10 June 1959.

Location: on the High Street.

Carnegie grant: £1,500 in 1910.

It was opened in 1913.

Description: a one-storey building of a simple Classical air.

Present use: no longer as a library.

DOLGELLAU, MERIONETH

National Records of Scotland, GD281/3/98 file, 9 October 1903–13 February 1957.

Location: on Mill Street; the site of the Old Blue Lion was paid for by subscription.

Carnegie grant: £1,000 in 1910.

Architect: E. A. Fermaud of London.

Contractor and builder: Edward Edwards.

The foundation stone was laid on 30 May 1911.

The library was opened in 1911.

Description: stucco with giant pilasters surmounted by an elaborate 'Darllenfa Rydd Dolgellau' (Dolgellau Free Library). The restoration of the building was completed in 2014.

Present use: as the town's library.

DOWLAIS BRANCH LIBRARY, GLAMORGAN

Location: on the south-east side of Upper Union Street, opposite St John's Church.

Carnegie grant: £1,500 in 1902.

Architect: E. A. Johnson of Abergavenny.

Contractor: T. A. Jones of Cardiff.

The branch library was opened in January 1907 by Sir D. Alfred Thomas MP.

Description: a Grade II listed building (Cadw 27083), in a free seventeenth-century style with Tudor/seventeenth-century carved art nouveau detail. Its two storeys are constructed of Pennant stone with red sandstone dressings. Internally, the main reading room retains its open timber roof.

Present use: as Dowlais's public library.

FLINT, FLINTSHIRE

National Records of Scotland, GD281/3/121 file, 13 April 1902–27 September 1904.

Location: on Market Square, in the lower part of the town hall.

Carnegie grant: £200 in 1903.

The library was opened in June 1903 by J. Herbert Lewis, MP.

Description: part of the market hall on the ground floor of the town hall (Cadw 14891) had space for 20,000 volumes.

Present use: as part of the town hall.

LLANDRINDOD WELLS, RADNORSHIRE
National Records of Scotland, GD281/3/201 file, 25 June 1902–6 February 1936.
Location: on Temple Street, next to the town hall.
Carnegie grant: £1,500 in 1906.
Description: it was founded as a library with one room for a museum.
Present use: as Radnorshire Museum.

LLANDUDNO, CAERNARFONSHIRE
National Records of Scotland, GD281/3/202 file, 21 September 1903–9 July 1927.
Location: on Mostyn Street; the site was provided by Lord Mostyn.
Carnegie grant: £4,000 in 1907.
Architect: G. A. Humphreys, architect of the Mostyn estate.
Contractor: Edward Owen.
The library was opened by Lord Mostyn in September 1910.
Description: a Grade II listed building (Cadw 25362): a two-storey building in Baroque style, of Bath stone. At the entrance is a circular mosaic with the town's name and crest; the first floor has a saucer-shaped dome set on Doric columns. The first-floor level facing the street housed the reference library, with Baroque detailing, a barrel-vaulted ceiling, medallion-cornice; paired pilasters frame an oriel window.
Present use: as Llandudno's town library.

MERTHYR TYDFIL CENTRAL LIBRARY, GLAMORGAN
Location: on the High Street.
Carnegie grant: £1,500 in 1902, later in the year increased to £2,500 to enable the purchase of the site of Shiloh chapel; the total sum was further increased to over £12,000 by 1905 for the central library and its six branch libraries.
Architect: Councillor T. Edmund of Messrs Johnson, Richards and Rees of Merthyr.
Contractor: Messrs Enoch Williams and Sons of Dowlais.
The central library was opened in 1935.
Description: a Grade II listed building in a modern Arts and Crafts style (Cadw 11442). It is of two storeys in Portland stone and with a slate roof.
Present use: as Merthyr Tydfil's central library.

CORPORATION ROAD BRANCH LIBRARY, NEWPORT, MONMOUTHSHIRE

National Records of Scotland, GD281/3/240 file, 16 September 1902–8 February 1907.

Location: on Corporation Road; the site was given by a Mr Morgan.

Carnegie grant: £2,000 in 1904.

Architect: C. F. Ward, the borough architect and surveyor of Newport.

Contractor: J. H. Williams.

The library was opened on 14 March 1907 by the mayor of Newport.

Description: built in an Edwardian Baroque style, in red brick with Bath stone dressings.

Present use: as a branch library until 2015.

PENARTH, GLAMORGAN

National Records of Scotland, GD281/3/287 file, 9 October 1901–29 August 1955.

Location: on the corner of Stanwell Road and Rectory Road; the site was provided by Lord Windsor of St Fagans.

Carnegie grant: £4,000 in 1903.

Architect: H. Snell, architect to the Windsor Estate.

Contractor: Messrs Turner and Sons of Cardiff.

The foundation stone was laid by Councillor Samuel Thomas, chairman of the library committee, in the absence of Lord Windsor, on 10 September 1904. The library was opened in 1905.

Description: a Grade II listed building (Cadw 13366). A two-storey building of free Jacobean style, constructed of grey rubble masonry with dressings. A boys' reading room was in the basement and a ladies' reading room on the first floor; the main reading room was on the ground floor. It has a clock tower to add to its distinction.

Present use: as Penarth's town library.

PENYDARREN BRANCH LIBRARY, GLAMORGAN

Location: the site was gifted by Alderman Thomas Williams JP of Gwaelod-y-garth.

Carnegie grant: £700 in 1902.

The library reading room was opened by Sir D. Alfred Thomas and Alderman Thomas Williams in September 1902, the first of Merthyr Tydfil's branch libraries to be completed.

Present use: unknown.

PONTYPOOL, MONMOUTHSHIRE
National Records of Scotland, GD281/3/255 file, 26 July 1903–15 August 1950.
Location: on Commercial Street; the site was given by John Capel Hanbury of Pontypool Park.
Carnegie grant: £2,000 in 1904.
Architect: Speir and Beavan of Cardiff.
Contractor: W. N. Campbell of Pontypool.
The library was opened on 21 September 1908 by John Capel Hanbury of Pontypool Park.
Description: a Grade II listed building (Cadw 18809). Of two storeys in an Edwardian Baroque style, it is constructed of red brick with Portland limestone dressings. It had a general reading room, a reference library, a lending library, a ladies' reading room, and a small lecture hall. The unaltered interior has a prominent stair leading from the central hall, which has some art nouveau-style stained glass.
Present use: as Pontypool's town library.

RHYL, FLINTSHIRE
National Records of Scotland, GD281/3/268 file, 18 July 1902–4 February 1955.
Location: on Wellington Road, adjacent to the town hall; the site was provided by the town council.
Carnegie grant: £3,000 in 1903 but not confirmed until 1905.
Architect: A. A. Goodall, the town surveyor.
Contractor: Messrs Jones and Pritchard of Abergele.
The foundation stone was laid in January 1906 by the high sheriff of Flintshire, W. J. P. Storye, and Councillor J. W. Jones, chairman of Rhyl urban district council.
The library was opened by Sir J. Herbert Lewis MP in April 1907.
Description: library and town hall are a Grade II listed building (Cadw 1498), of Penmaenmawr stone facing with Cefn stone dressings. The ground floor of the library had a reading room for 80–100 readers, a reference room, a lending area and a librarian's room; there was space for 10,000–12,000 volumes. On the first floor were a hall and dressing rooms.
Present use: as town council offices.

ROGERSTONE, MONMOUTHSHIRE

National Records of Scotland, GD281/3/270 file, 10 October 1902–1 June 1904.

Location: on Tregwilym Road; the site was gifted by Lord Tredegar.

Carnegie grant: £1,400 in 1903.

Architect: Messrs Swash and Bain of Newport.

Contractor: C. H. Read of Newport.

The library was opened on 4 November 1905 by Lord Tredegar.

Description: a Grade II listed building (Cadw 81345). In an Edwardian free Classical style, it is of squared purple sandstone with a slate roof and a lantern dome. It has contemporary imitation marble fireplaces.

Present use: as Rogerstone's public library.

SKEWEN (OR COEDFRANC), GLAMORGAN

National Records of Scotland, GD281/3/291 file, 27 September 1902– 31 March 1970.

Location: Evelyn Road, Skewen; the site was donated by Winifred Coombe Tennant and the Tennant trustees.

Carnegie grant: £2,000.

Architect: J. Cook Rees of Neath.

Contractor: Messrs Price Bros.

The foundation stone was laid in 1904.

The library was opened in June 1905 by the wife of Sir Samuel Thomas Evans MP.

Description: semi-Baroque in style, with tomato-coloured brick and mustard-coloured terracotta stone.

Present use: as a community hall; in March 2020 it also became Skewen's public library once again.

TAI-BACH, MARGAM, GLAMORGAN

Location: Commercial Road, Tai-bach; the site was gifted by Emily Talbot and the Margam Estate.

Carnegie grant: £2,500 in 1913.

Architect: John Cox, district surveyor for Margam urban district council.

Contractor: Messrs J. Vaughan John of Port Talbot.

The foundation stone was laid on 18 July 1914 by Councillor William Lewis.

The library was opened in June 1916 by Councillor William Lewis.

Description: a Grade II listed building (Cadw 22807). A two-storey building in Classical style, of grey Pennant stone with pale Bath stone dressings.

The entrance area has a tiled floor and moulded ceiling. The main reading room was on the ground floor; it also had a juvenile library, and a reference and magazine room, with a ladies' reading room and a large hall on the first floor.

Present use: as a community facility and library.

For an account of the library, see Hughes, 'The history of libraries in the Port Talbot district', 127–31.

TRECYNON, GLAMORGAN

National Records of Scotland, GD281/3/328 file, 12 October 1901–28 April 1947.

Location: on Mill St, facing the Square.

Carnegie grant: £1,000, supplemented by local coal owners and public subscription.

Architect: C. H. Elford.

Contractor: Tyssul Davies.

The foundation stone of Trecynon Public Hall and Library was laid on 30 August 1902 by Lord Windsor of St Fagans, D. Alfred Thomas MP and Rees Llewelyn of Bwllfa House, Cwmdare.

The public hall and library were opened on 10 March 1903.

Description: a large, prominent, two-storey yet simple structure that incorporated both library and a public hall.

Present use: various community and commercial activities.

TREHARRIS BRANCH LIBRARY, GLAMORGAN

Location: on Perrott Street; the site was provided by the owners of the Pantannas Estate.

Carnegie grant: £700 in 1902, subsequently raised to £1,750.

Architect: William Dowdeswell of Treharris.

Contractor: Frank Ekers of Newport.

The branch library was opened in October 1909 by Andrew Wilson, the mayor of Merthyr Tydfil.

Description: a Grade II listed building in a free Edwardian style (Cadw 80909). It is of red brick and Bath stone dressings. The entrance recess has a mosaic floor with 'CL' in a wreath (for Carnegie Library); the decorated stained-glass windows and the carved librarian's kiosk remain in situ; a contemporary art nouveau plaque records the library's opening. It had space for 3,600 volumes.

Present use: as Treharris's town library.

TROEDYRHIW BRANCH LIBRARY, GLAMORGAN
Location: on Tyntaldwyn Road; the site was gifted by Lord Windsor of St Fagans.
Carnegie grant: £700 in 1902.
Description: a small one-storey building, with tall neo-Gothic windows.
Present use: vacant but recently restored.

WHITCHURCH, CARDIFF
National Records of Scotland, GD281/3/346 file, 7 July 1902–14 April 1954.
Location: at the junction of Merthyr Road and Velindre Road; the site had been acquired by Whitchurch parish council from the Ecclesiastical Commissioners in 1899.
Carnegie grant: £2,000 in 1902 (though the *Weekly Mail,* December 1904, says £3,000).
Architect: R. and S. Williams of Cardiff.
Contractor: W. T. Morgan.
The library was opened on 14 December 1904 by Councillor A. H. Bullock, chairman of the library committee.
Description: a Grade II listed building (Cadw 26715). Of Flemish Baroque style of the seventeenth century, it was built of red brick with Bath stone dressings and a Welsh slate roof. A room at the east end of the library was designated as a ladies' reading room; at the west end space for games was set aside in 1905 'as an experiment'.
Present use: as Whitchurch public library.

WREXHAM, DENBIGHSHIRE
National Records of Scotland, GD281/3/354 file, 8 October 1902–2 November 1911.
Location: on Queen's Square, a site provided by Wrexham borough council.
Carnegie grant: £4,000 in 1903, to which was added a further £300 in October 1906.
Architect: Vernon Hodge of Teddington, London.
Contractor: Mr Robert Roweley of Gresford.
The foundation stone was laid by the mayoress of Wrexham, Mrs Birkett Evans, on 1 January 1906.
The library was opened by Sir Foster Cunliffe of Acton Hall on 15 February 1907. For a programme of the opening ceremony, see Denbighshire Archives DD/G/2207.

Description: a Grade II listed building (Cadw 1852). Of two storeys in an Edwardian Baroque style, the ground floor is of stone with red brick above. It has a small square cupola and the central window has a cartouche. Internally, the ground floor had a ladies' room to seat *c.*20, a reference room, a general reading room for *c.*50 and a lending library; on the upper floor there was a lecture hall that could seat 200. There was space for *c.*20,000 volumes.

Librarian: Richard Gough, 1879–1911.

For an account of the library, see Dodd, *A History of Wrexham, Denbighshire,* pp. 120, 130–1, 332.

Present use: as council offices (since 1972).

SELECTED IMAGES OF THE
CARNEGIE LIBRARIES OF WALES

Figure 13. Abergavenny, Monmouthshire, front entrance elevation.

Figure 14. Aberystwyth, Cardiganshire (*wikimedia.org/Stefanik* CC BY-SA 4.0).

Figure 15. Bangor, Caernarfonshire, entrance elevation (*www.mikepeel.net* CC BY-SA 4.0).

Figure 16. Barry, Glamorgan, with the clock tower and new town hall added (left) (© Ferguson Mann Architects, Bristol).

Figure 17. Bridgend, Glamorgan.

Figure 18.   Brynmawr, Monmouthshire, c.1907. An early photograph of the library built on a virgin site donated by the Duke of Beaufort. It was opened in October 1905, and although its purpose has changed the structure of the building has been little altered since then (National Library of Wales).

Figure 19.   Buckley, Flintshire, with the new town hall added (left).

Figure 20. Canton, Cardiff, Glamorgan, the Library Street elevation (*wikimedia.org/Jaggery* CC BY-SA 2.0).

Figure 21. Cathays, Cardiff, Glamorgan, the distinctive 'butterfly' entrance elevation (*wikimedia.org/John Lord* (© Crown copyright: RCAHMW; reproduced with the permission of The Royal Commission on the Ancient and Historical Monuments of Wales, under delegated authority from The Keeper of the Public Records).

Figure 22. Church Village, Glamorgan.

Figure 23. Coedpoeth, Denbighshire, an oblique photograph of the front elevation.

Figure 24. Colwyn Bay, Caernarfonshire, an oblique photograph of the entrance elevation.

Figure 25. Deiniolen, Caernarfonshire (from the collections of the National Monuments Record of Wales © Richard Hayman).

Figure 26. Dolgellau, Merioneth, photographed prior to renovation in 2014 (© Rhys Llwyd Davies Architects, Bala).

Figure 27. Dowlais, Glamorgan, the entrance elevation on a hillside site (*wikimedia.org/John Lord* CC BY-SA 2.0).

Figure 28. Llandrindod Wells, Radnorshire, the entrance elevation.

Figure 29. Llandudno, Caernarfonshire, front elevation (*wikimedia.org/Paul the archivist* CC BY-SA 4.0).

Figure 30. Merthyr Tydfil, with the statue of H. S. Berry, Lord Buckland (1931), in the foreground.

Figure 31. Corporation Road, Newport, Monmouthshire.

Figure 32. Penarth, the original entrance elevation on Stanwell Road.

Figure 33. Pontypool, Monmouthshire (© Crown copyright: RCAHMW; reproduced with the permission of The Royal Commission on the Ancient and Historical Monuments of Wales, under delegated authority from The Keeper of the Public Records).

Figure 34. Rogerstone, front elevation with the entrance to the left.

Figure 35.   Skewen, Glamorgan, an oblique photograph of the front elevation.

Figure 36. Trecynon, Glamorgan.

Figure 37.   Treharris, Glamorgan.

Figure 38.   Whitchurch, Glamorgan, front elevation, with the Whitchurch war memorial (1920) in the foreground (*wikimedia.org/Motacilla* CC BY-SA 3.0).

Figure 39.   Wrexham, Denbighshire (*wikimedia.org/Rept0n1x* CC BY-SA 3.0).

LIST OF SOURCES

WORKS OF REFERENCE

British Listed Buildings, *https://britishlistedbuildings.co.uk/wales*

J. A. Garraty and M. C. Carnes (eds), *American National Biography*, 24 vols (New York and Oxford, 1999)

J. E. Lloyd and R. T. Jenkins (eds), *The Dictionary of Welsh Biography Down to 1940* (London, 1959), revised *https://biography.wales/*

H. C. G. Matthew (ed.), *Oxford Dictionary of National Biography* (Oxford, 2004) and *http://www.oxforddnb.com*

The Royal Commission on the Ancient and Historical Monuments of Wales, *www.coflein.org.uk*

UNPUBLISHED ARCHIVES

Ceredigion Archives, ABM/SE/1/5, 6
Conwy Archives, CMostyn Estate Plans, 7 and 8
Denbighshire Archives, DD/G/2207047
Denbighshire Archives, DD/G/2207044–5
Denbighshire Archives, PCD/6/136
Flintshire Record Office, D-DM/1109/1–9, 11, 16–27; D-DM/1109/D/5
Glamorgan Archives, BB/C/3/34, 39–40

Glamorgan Archives, BC/5/1/16234
Glamorgan Archives, BCOW/C/96/24
Glamorgan Archives, DXDQ
Glamorgan Archives, P6/62
Gwent Archives, A320/M/7, 8
Gwent Archives, Abergavenny Borough Council, D894/19
Gwent Archives, Abergavenny Library Papers, D1348/11, 5, 8, 6, 9, 13, 14,
    18, 20, 22
Gwent Archives, Rogerstone Parish Council, D385/1
Gwent Archives, D454/1403
Gwent Archives, Pontypool Parish Council, A433/M/12, 13
Gwent Archives, Newport Borough Council, A110/A/M/13, 14
National History Museum at St Fagans, Accession no. F91.30
National Library of Wales MS 19440E
National Library of Wales, UNC/1
National Library of Wales, Welsh Newspapers Online, *https://newspapers.
    library.wales/*
National Library of Wales, William George (Solicitor) Papers
National Records of Scotland, GD281/3
Powys Archives, R/X 137/10 and RC/A/1/309
Royal Commission on the Ancient and Historical Monuments of Wales
West Glamorgan Archives, D/D T958
West Glamorgan Archives, NPT/42 (1915)
West Glamorgan Archives, SL Lib. 5/2, 5/3

NEWSPAPERS

Aberdare Leader
Abergavenny Chronicle
Barry Dock News
Barry Herald
The Big Issue
*The Brecon Radnor Express, Carmarthen and Swansea Valley Gazette and
    Brynmawr District Advertiser*
Caerphilly Journal
The Cambria Daily Leader
Cambrian News
Cambrian News and Merionethshire Standard

The Cardiff Times
The Carnarvon and Denbigh Herald and North and South Wales Independent
Cheshire Observer
The Chester Courant and Advertiser for North Wales
The County Echo
County Observer and Monmouthshire Central Advertiser
The Evening Express
Glamorgan Gazette
The Guardian
Llandudno Advertiser and List of Visitors
Merthyr Express
North Wales Chronicle
The North Wales Express
The Observer
The Pembrokeshire County Guardian and Cardigan Reporter
The Pembrokeshire Herald and General Advertiser
Prestatyn Weekly
The Public Library Journal
Rhyl Journal
Rhyl Record and Advertiser
Weekly Mail
The Weekly News and Visitors' Chronicle for Colwyn Bay
The Welsh Coast Pioneer and Review for North Cambria
Welsh Gazette and West Wales Advertiser
Wrexham Advertiser

PUBLISHED WRITINGS

S. Awbery, *Let Us Talk of Barry* ([Barry], 1954)

C. M. Baggs, '"Carnegie offered money and a lot of south Wales refused to have it: it was blood money": Bringing public libraries to the south Wales valleys, 1870–1939', *Library History*, 17 (November 2001), 171–9

A. Bowen, *The History of the Libraries in the Borough of Merthyr Tydfil and District, 1846-1946* (Merthyr Tydfil, n.d.)

R.W. Burnie (ed.), *Memoir and Letters of Sidney Gilchrist Thomas, Inventor* (London, 1891)

J. W. P. Campbell, *The Library: A World History* (London, 2013)

A. Carnegie, 'Wealth', *North American Review*, CXLVIII (June 1889) and CXLIX (December 1889)

A. Carnegie, *The Gospel of Wealth and Other Timely Essays*, ed. E. C. Kirkland (Cambridge, MA, 1965)

A. Crawford (ed.), *The Meaning of the Library: A Cultural History* (Princeton and Oxford, 2015)

The Criccieth Heritage Walk, 2nd edn (Criccieth, 2003)

D. J. Davies, *Ninety Years of Endeavour: The Tredegar Workmen's Hall, 1861–1951* (Cardiff, 1951)

A. H. Dodd, *A History of Wrexham, Denbighshire* (Wrexham, 1957)

A. Donaldson and I. Macleod, 'Andrew Carnegie: The injustice of ranks and the crisis of wealth', *Merthyr Historian*, 14 (2002), 167–86

H. Edwards, *Capel Llanelli: Our Rich Heritage* (Carmarthen, 2009)

J. Edwards, *Llanelli: Story of a Town* (for *The Llanelli Star*, Derby, 2001)

E. L. Ellis, *The University College of Wales, Aberystwyth, 1872–1972* (Cardiff, 1972)

T. Gage, *American Prometheus: Carnegie's Captain, Bill Jones* (Arcata, CA, 2017)

A. Giridharadas, *Winners Take All* (London, 2019)

S. Goodenough, *The Greatest Good Fortune: Andrew Carnegie's Gift for Today* (Edinburgh, 1985)

T. E. Griffiths, 'Caernarvonshire and its libraries: development of the first county library in Wales', *Transactions of the Caernarvonshire Historical Society*, 33 (1972), 170–89

A. Grimes, *Irish Carnegie Libraries: A Catalogue and Architectural History* (Dublin, 1998)

A. M. Hacker, *The World of Andrew Carnegie, 1865–1901* (Philadelphia and New York, 1968)

R. Hanbury-Tennison, *The Hanburys of Monmouthshire* (privately printed, Aberystwyth, 1995)

B. Harrison, 'William George Stewart Adams (1874–1966)', in *ODNB, s.n.*

C. Harvey, H. Maclean, J. Gordon and E. Shaw, 'Andrew Carnegie and the foundations of contemporary entrepreneurial philanthropy', *Business History*, 53/3 (2011), 425–50

B. J. Hendrick, *The Life of Andrew Carnegie* (London, 1932)

F. P. Hill, *James Bertram: An Appreciation* (New York, 1936)

History of the Libraries in the Borough of Merthyr Tydfil and District, 1846–1946 (Merthyr Tydfil, n.d.)

E. Hubbard, *The Buildings of Wales: Clwyd* (London, 1986)

'The Centenary of Coedpoeth Library', compiled by D. Hughes and P. Jeorrett (Coedpoeth Community Council, n.d.)

J.V. Hughes, 'The history of libraries in the Port Talbot district', *Transactions of the Port Talbot History Society*, 4/2 (2000), 108–37

P. H. Jones, 'Public libraries in Wales since 1862', in A. Black and P. Hoare (eds), *The Cambridge History of Libraries in Britain and Ireland* (Cambridge, 2006), pp. 216–26

W. D. Jones, *Wales in America; Scranton and the Welsh, 1860–1920* (Cardiff, 1993)

T. Kelly, *History of Public Libraries in Great Britain, 1845–1975* (London, 1977)

M. Klein, *The Change Makers: From Carnegie to Gates, How the Great Entrepreneurs Transformed Ideas into Industries* (New York, 2003)

J. Knight, *Blaenavon: From Iron Town to World Heritage Site* (Wooton Almeley, 2016)

E. C. Lagemann, *The Politics of Knowledge: The Carnegie Corporation, Philanthropy and Public Policy* (Chicago, 1992)

W. J. Lewis, *Born on a Perilous Rock: Aberystwyth Past and Present* (Aberystwyth, 1980)

T. Lloyd, J. Orbach and R. Scourfield, *The Buildings of Wales: Carmarthenshire and Ceredigion* (New Haven and London, 2006)

J. Mackay, *Little Boss: A Life of Andrew Carnegie* (Edinburgh and London, 1997)

D. Moore (ed.), *Barry: The Centenary Book* (Barry, 1984; 2nd revised edn 1988)

W. A. Munford, *A History of the Library Association, 1877–1977* (London, 1976)

D. Nasaw, *Andrew Carnegie* (London, 2006)

J. Newman, *The Buildings of Wales: Glamorgan* (London, 1995)

J. Piggott, 'Clive, Robert George Windsor, Baron Windsor and earl of Plymouth (1857–1925)', in *ODNB, s.n.*

E. Price, *Lloyd George a'r eisteddfod genedlaethol a phrifwyliau Bangor a Chaernarfon* (Caernarfon, 2005)

O. Prizeman, *Philanthropy and Light: Carnegie Libraries and the Advent of Transatlantic Standards for Public Space* (Farnham, 2012)

J. Randall, *Our Coal and Iron Industries, and the Men who have Wrought in Connection with them: The Wilkinsons* (Madeley, 1879)

'Edward Windsor Richards', *https://www.imeche.org*

W. Robertson, *Welfare in Trust: A History of the Carnegie United Kingdom Trust, 1913–1963* (Dunfermline, 1964)

P. Rowland, *Lloyd George* (London, 1975)

D. S. Scott, *Public Library Development in Glamorgan, 1920 to 1974: An Area Study with Particular Reference to Glamorgan County Library* (Library Association, 1979)

D. Sellwood, 'The libraries that never were', *The Journal of the Caerphilly Local History Society*, 8 (2007), 28–35

P. Stead, *Coleg Harlech: The First Fifty Years* (Cardiff, 1977)

A. Thompson, *Library Buildings of Britain and Europe* (London, 1963)

P. F. Tobin, 'Pontypridd Public Library, 1890–1990', in P. F. Tobin and J. I. Davies (eds), *The Bridge and the Song: Some Chapters in the Story of Pontypridd* (Bridgend, 1991), pp. 66–77

G. Tweedale, 'Andrew Carnegie (1835–1919)', in H. C. G. Matthew (ed.), *Oxford Dictionary of National Biography* (Oxford, 2004), and *http://www.oxforddnb.com*

J. C. van Dyke (ed.), *Autobiography of Andrew Carnegie* (New York, 1920, 2006)

J. F. Wall, *Andrew Carnegie*, 2nd edn (Pittsburgh, 1989)

UNPUBLISHED THESES

C. M. Baggs, 'The miners' libraries of South Wales from the 1860s to 1939' (unpublished PhD thesis, Aberystwyth University, 2 vols, 1995)

J. Roe, 'The Public Library in Wales: its history and development in the context of local government' (unpublished MA thesis, Queen's University Belfast, 1970)

INDEX

Entries in *italics* refer to the captions
of illustrations

Aberaman, 77
Aberavon, 45
Abercanaid library, 2–4, 44, 49, 56, 64,
    105
Abercynon, 77
Aberdare, 66, 78
    Valley, 62, 66
Aberdeen University, 81
Aberfan library, 2–3, 49, 56, 105
Abergavenny
    freedom of, 58, 68, 97, 106
    Holy Trinity Church, 55, 106
    library, 2–4, *23*, 26, 39, 41, 43, 55–9,
        61, 63–4, 68, 106, *120*
    marquess of, 55–8, 106
    museum, 59
    Royal Electrograph and Palace of
        Varieties, 63
    town of, 68
    mayor 106; *see also* Williams, W.

Abersychan, 74–5
    urban district, 74–5
Aberystwyth, 64, 92
    assembly rooms, 22
    borough council, 106
    mayor of, 67
    library, 2–4, 21–2, 27, 39, 41, 44–5,
        52, 55, 58, 61, 64, 71, *86*, *87*,
        108–7, *121*
    literary society, 21–2
Acton, Lord, 52
Adams, W. G. S., 84
Afon Lwyd Valley, 74
Allegheny, Penn., 15–16
Allen, Miss, of Beaumaris, 22
Amalgamated Society of Carpenters
    and Joiners of Abergavenny, 39
American Bessemer Steel Association,
    27
American Civil War, 26
Anderson, Col. James, 15–16, 90
Architects, 35, 39, 43, 52–4, 57–8,
    105–19

Art Nouveau, 52, 55, 106–7, 109–12, 115, 117
Australia libraries, 23

Ballinger, John, 68–9, *87*, 99
Bangor
    city council, 107
    eisteddfod, 28
    library, 2–4, 22, 28, 41, 54–5, *67*, 68, 96, 107, *122*
    University College of North Wales, 28
Barmouth, English Presbyterian Church, 83
Barry, 42
    government buildings, 53
    library, 2–4, 13, 23, 35, 43, 53, 55, 57, 68, 93–4, 107, *122*
    post office building, 53
    town council, 107
    town hall, 107
    Welsh Congregational Chapel, 13–14
Bates, E. K., of Newport, architect, 108
Beaufort, 9th duke of, 47, 95, 108, *124*
    wife of, 47
Beaumaris library, 22
Beaumont Thomas Works of Cwmbwrla, 73
Berry, H. S., Lord Buckland, *132*
Bersham, 41–2, 62; *see also* Coedpoeth
Bertram, James, 8, 14, 23, 25, 33–6, 44, 46–7, 49, 51–2, 56, 58–9, 66, 69, 72–4, 76, 78, 82–3, 93–4, 96, 98–9
    library guidance , 35–6
Bessemer medal, 29
Bessemer process, 8, 26–7, 49
Bible, The, 83
Big Issue, The, 5
Birmingham, 39, 42
Blaenavon, 27
    Calvinistic Methodist Church, 83

Blaenau Ffestiniog library, 20–1
Board of Education, 30
Boer War, The, 66
Books and magazines, 46–7, 50–1, 59–62, 66, 68, 75, 84–5, 91, 95, 98, 107–8, 110–12, 115, 117
    catalogues, 64
    English and Welsh literature, 62–4
    history and travel, 62–4
    religion, 62–4
    science and mining, 62–4
Boulton, Matthew, 42
Bradley, A. G., 63
Brecon, 25, 78–9, 92
    library, 20, 78–9, 85
    literary institute, 78
Breconshire, 28, 43, 78–9, 85
    county council, 79
    deputy-lieutenant of, 47;
        see also Beaufort, duke of
Bridgend
    library, 2–4, 21, 41–3, 46, 68, 108, *123*
    mechanics' institution, 21
    town council, 46
British Army, 33
British West Indies libraries, 23
Broughton library, 21
Brynmawr
    library, 2–4, 41, 43, 47, 71, 108, *124*
    institute, 47, 108
Buckland, Lord, *see* Berry
Buckley
    library, 2–4, 42, 45, 108–9, *124*
    town hall, 108–9, *124*
    vicar of, and wife, 45
Buffett, Warren E., 15
Bullock, Councillor A. H., 118

Caernarfon: chapel organ, 83
    eisteddfod, 28, 87
    library, 20

Caernarfonshire
    county architect, 54
    county library, 86
    lord lieutenant of, *see* Greaves
Caerphilly, 75–6
    'library question', 75–6
    urban district council, 75–6
    workmen's institutes, 75–7, 97
Cambrian Railway Company, 45
Campbell, W. N., of Pontypool,
    contractor, 53, 115
Campbell-Bannerman, Henry, prime
    minister, 52
Canada libraries, 23
Canton library, 2–3, 36, 53, 59–61,
    68–9, 72, 98, 109, *125*
Cardiff, 41, *42*, 52-4, *87*
    central library, 20–1, 72
    city hall and law courts, 53
    town (and city) council, 72, 109
    lord mayor of, 69, 109
Cardiganshire
    county library, 86–7
    MP for, *see* Davies, M. L. V.
Carnarvon Boroughs, MP for, 28;
    see also Lloyd George, David
Carnegie, Andrew
    early life, 7–8, 16
    brother, 7, 27
    father, 82
    mother, 16
    death, 8
    wife, Louise Whitfield, 8
    daughter, Margaret, 8–9, 28, *86*,
        87, 90
    portraits, *frontispiece, 9*, 56–7, 97
    business interests, 4, 7–8
    educational interests, 81–2
    musical interests, 23, 28, 82–4;
        see also organs
    philanthropy, 2–4, 8, 11–16, 23, 41,
        43–4, 56, 71, 81, 84

social attitudes, 12–16
    writings, 12, 15–16, 42–3;
        see also Gospel of Wealth
    and Wales, 25–30, 49, 58
    legacy, 81-7
Carnegie Bros and Co., 8
Carnegie Corporation of New York,
    34, 83, 85
Carnegie Endowment for
    International Peace, 84
Carnegie Steel Trust, 108–9
Carnegie Trust for Universities in
    Scotland, 81
Carnegie United Kingdom Trust, 4, 50,
    82, 83–5, 87
Carroll, Lewis, 62
Cathays library, 2–4, 38, 53, 56, 58–60,
    60, 68–9, 72, 109, *125*
Cathays Park, 53
Cawdor, earl of, 20
Chester, 45
    free library, 61
Church Village library, 2–3, 27, 54–7,
    66, 110, *126*
Churchill, Lord Randolph, 62
Coedffranc, *see* Skewen
Coedpoeth (or Bersham)
    library, 2–3, 41, 61–2, 65, 71, 110,
        127
    Welsh Wesleyan Methodist
        Church, 82
Coleg Harlech, 82
Colwyn Bay library, 2–4, 35–6, 45, 54,
    58, 65, 110–11, *128*
Connah's Quay, 76
Conservative Party, 46
Contractors and Builders, 39, 52–4
Corstophine, Scotland, 33
Cowbridge, 51
    borough council, 51, 96
Cox, John, architect, 54, 116–17

Cricieth
    library, 2–3, 29, 43, 45, 54–6, 59,
        62–3, 111
    urban district council, 45, 62, 111
Cunliffe, Sir Foster, of Acton Hall,
    66–7, 99, 118
Cwm, near Pontypool, 74
Cynon Valley, 77

Davies, David, of Llandinam, MP, 27,
    64, 76–7, 106
Davies, Matthew Lewis Vaughan, of
    Tanybwlch, MP, 64, 106
    wife of, 64, 106
Davies, R. Cecil, architect, 108–9
Davies, Tyssul, contractor, 117
Defoe, Daniel, 62
Deiniolen library, 2–3, 41, 58, 111, 129
Denbighshire East, MP for, see
    Moss, S.
Denbighshire West, MP for, see
    Roberts, J. H.
Dixon and Potter, architects, 54, 107
Dolgellau library, 2–4, 20, 112, 129
Dowdeswell, William, architect, 50,
    53, 117
Dowlais, 27, 29, 46
    library, 2–3, 49, 55, 63, 66, 112, 130
    St John's Church, 112
Dowlais Iron Company, 49
Dunfermline, 7, 85
    library, 16
Dunraven: castle, 46
    earl of, 46, 108
    Estate 108
Dyfi estuary, 76

Ebbw Vale steel works, 29
Ebbw Valley, 46
Ecclesiastical Commissioners, 118
Edgar Thomas Steelworks,
    Pennsylvania, 26

Edinburgh, 33
    Daniel Stewart's College, 33
    library, 16, 69
    University, 81
Edmund, Councillor T., architect, 113
Edward VII, King, 111
Edward, James, of Llandrindod Wells,
    14
Edwards Bros, of Trefechan,
    contractors, 39, 106
Edwards, Edward, contractor, 112
Edwards, O. M., 68
Eisteddfodau, 13, 28, 92;
    see also Bangor, Caernarfon
Ekers, Frank, of Newport, contractor,
    53, 117
Elford, C. H., architect, 117
Eliot, George, 62
Evans, Mrs Birkett, of Wrexham, 66,
    118
Evans, David, of Cricieth, contractor,
    111
Evans, Messrs Robert, and Sons, of
    Old Conwy, contractor, 97, 111
Evans, Sir Samuel Thomas, MP, 27,
    63, 98, 116
    wife of, 63, 98

Fermaud, E.A., of London, architect,
    112
Fiji libraries, 23
First World War, 46, 49–50, 84, 93
Flint
    library, 2–3, 30, 44, 64, 95, 99, 112
    town hall, 44, 112
Flintshire, 62, 76
    high sheriff of, 65–6, 115;
        see also Storye, W. J. P.
    MP for, see Lewis, J. H.
Francis, B. J., 39, 94, 106
Frick, Henry Clay, 8, 26

Garndiffaith, 74–5
Gaskell, Mrs, 62
Gates, Bill, 15
Gilchrist, Percy, 27, 49
Gladstone, Herbert, 42, 45
Gladstone, W. E., prime minister, 15,
    27–8, 39, 72, 82
Glamorgan, 47, 54, 75, 87, 91
    lord lieutenant, 46, 68
    Mid, MP for, see Evans, S. J.
Glasgow, 52
    University, 81
Golden Grove, Carmarthenshire, 20
Goodall, A. A., architect, 115
Gorseinon, 78
Gospel of Wealth, 12–15
Gough, Richard, librarian, 119
Great Depression, 8
Great Northern and North-eastern
    Railway Company, South Africa,
    33
Greaves, J. E., 62–3, 111
Gresford, 118
Griffiths, Alderman Nathan, of
    Llanelli, 14–15
Griffiths, Robert and Thomas, of
    Chester, 45, 108–9
Griffithstown, 74
Guest, Keen and Nettlefolds, 49

Hague, The: Peace Palace, 84, 101
Halkyn newsroom, 22
Hanbury, John Capel, of Pontypool
    Park, 47, 75, 95–6, 115
Hardie, James K., 94
Harding, Councillor F. W., of New
    Inn, 74
Harvey, T. F., architect, 105
Harvey and Arshby, of Birmingham,
    designer, 109
Haverfordwest, 51–2: castle, 51–2

Hawarden, 29, 42, 45
    free library, 61
    St Deiniol's library, 27–8, 42
Herbert, Miss Rachel, Charity, of
    Abergavenny, 106
Hill, F. P., 93
Hodge, Vernon, of Teddington,
    architect, 52, 96, 118–19
Holyhead library, 21
Holywell, 44
Homestead strike, 8, 15, 73, 90
Honourable Society of
    Cymmrodorion, 68
House of Commons, 30, 93
House of Lords, 29
Hughes, Alderman Edward, of
    Wrexham, 42–3, 94–5, 99
Hughes and Stirling, of Liverpool,
    contractors, 54, 107
Humphreys, G. A., architect, 53–4,
    113
Hutchinson and Payne, architects, 53,
    107

India, secretary of state for, 52;
    see also Morley, John
Internationalism, 84
Ireland libraries, 23, 25, 89, 96
Iron works, 42
Iron and Steel Institute of Great
    Britain, 28, 46

Jenkins, John, of Brynmawr,
    contractor, 108
Jenkins, Revd John, of Church Village,
    100
Jenkins, Simon, 5
Jersey, earl of, 72–3
John, J. Vaughan, of Port Talbot,
    contractor, 47, 116–17
Johnson, E. A., of Abergavenny,
    architect, 112

Johnson, Richards and Rees, Messrs, of Merthyr Tydfil, architects, 113
Jones and Pritchard, Messrs, of Abergele, contractor, 115
Jones, Revd John, 25
Jones, Captain John, 22, *67*, 107
Jones, J. T., of Parciau, 45, 111
Jones, Councillor J. W., of Rhyl, 115
Jones, T. A., of Cardiff, 109, 112
Jones, Captain William (Bill) Richard, 25–8, 92

Kenfig reading room, 21

Lanchester, Henry Vaughan, architect, 53
Landore, Swansea, 73
League of Nations, 84
Lenox, Mass., 8
Lewis, J. Herbert, MP, 27, 29–30, 44, 64, *65*, 65–6, 84, 95, 99, 112, 115
Lewis, Councillor William, 116–17
Liberal Party, 27, 51–2, 64, 66
Librarians, 5, 36, 43, *60*, 119
Libraries
    accommodation, for children, 36–8, 59–60, *60*, 98, 109, 117, 119
    for women, 19, 23, 36–8, 59, 98, 109, 115, 119
    endowed, 11, 19–20
    fittings and furniture, 37, 58–64, 98
    lighting and heating, 37, 61, 72
    public movement, 4, 11, 21, 85–7
    sites, 43–52
    subscription, 11, 19–20
Libraries (architecture)
    styles, 52–8
    Arts and Crafts, 52, 53, 55–66, 108–9, 113
    Baroque, 52, 55, 107, 108, 113–16, 118–19

Classical, 52, 54–5, 106, 111, 116–17
    Gothic, 52, 55–6, 105–6, 118
    Jacobean, 114
    Renaissance, 52, 54, 56, 110
Library Association of Great Britain, 29–30, 47, 66, 68, 84
Literacy, 19; *see also* Books and magazines
Literary and scientific societies, 19–20
Liverpool, 52, 107
    Cunard building, 52
Llanberis library, 20–1
Llanddeiniolen, *see* Deiniolen
Llandeilo-Talybont parish council, 78
Llandrindod Wells
    library, 2–3, 14, 41, 113, *131*
    town hall, 113
Llandudno library, 2–3, 20, 36, 41, 45, 53–5, 68, 113, *132*
Llanelli, 14
    Athenaeum, 20
    Capel Newydd, 83
    library, 20–1
    mechanics' institute, 20–1, 91
Llanidloes, 76
Llanrhaeadr-ym-Mochnant: parish church, 83
    vicar of, *see* Morgan, William
Llantwit Fardre, *see* Church Village
Llewelyn, Rees, of Bwllfa House, Cwmdare, 117
Lloyd, John, of Brecon and London, 36, 78–9, 85
Lloyd George, David, MP, 27–9, 43, 46, 66, 86, 93, 98
    brother, William, 29, 86
London, 29, 53–4, 68, 78
    lord mayor, 106; *see also* Morgan, Sir Walter V.

Machynlleth library, 76 7; *see also*
     Owen Glendower Institute
Manchester, 54, 107, 111
     library, 20
Margam Abbey Estate, 45–6, 116–17
Margam
     urban district council, 45–6, 54,
          116–17; *see also* Tai-bach
Massachusetts, 8
Matthews, Alderman W. P., 67
Mauritius library, 23
Mechanics' Institutions 19–21
Merioneth, 83
Merthyr Tydfil, 29, 42, 48–9
     branch libraries, *frontispiece*, 66, 78
     central library, 2–3, 20, 25, 29,
          48–50, 113, *132*
     mayor, *50*, 117; *see also* Wilson, A.
     MP, *see* Thomas, D. A.
     Shiloh Welsh Wesleyan Chapel,
          49, 113
     urban district council, 44, 48, 105
Midlothian, MP for, *see* Gladstone,
     W. E.
Milford Haven, St Katherine's Church,
     83
Miller, Roswell, Jr, *86*, *87*
     wife of, *see* Carnegie, Margaret
Miners' libraries and institutes, 19, 21,
     41, 77–8, 87, 100
Minerva, representation of, 55, 57
Monmouthshire, 91
     deputy lieutenant, 46
     lord lieutenant, 46
Montgomeryshire
     MP, *see* Davies, David
Morgan, J. P., 4
Morgan, Sir Walter Vaughan, 28, 106
Morgan, Dr William, 83
Morgan, W. T., of Cardiff, contractor,
     109, 118
Morley, John, 51–2

Morrison, Hew, of Edinburgh, 69, 109
Morriston, Swansea, 73
Moss, Samuel, MP, 65, 110
Moss, Samuel, contractor, 110
Moss, William, architect, 110
Mostyn: Estate, 54
     Lord, 45, 54, 68, 113
Mountain Ash, 77–8
     miners' library, 77
     urban district council, 87, 102

Natal Government Railways, 33
National Assembly for Wales, 4
National History Museum of Wales, 98
National Library of Wales, 44, *87*, 96,
     99
National Museum for Wales, 66
Neath, 46, 63
     mechanics' institute, 21
Newcastle Emlyn library, 21
New Inn, 74; *see also* Harding, F. W.
Newport, 20–1, 41, 52–3, 72, 114
     borough architect, 54, 115
     Corporation Road library, 2–3, 36,
          54, 58, 72, *133*
     town of, 46, 72
     mayor, 63, 72, 114
New York, 7–8, 23, 27–8, 47, 73, 76,
     85, 93
     Carnegie mansion, 8, 34, 82
New Zealand library, 23
North American Review, 12

Organs, Church and Chapel, 82–5
Ogmore library, 21
O'Reilly Telegraph Company, 7
Oswestry, 39
Owen, Daniel, novelist, 62
Owen, Edward, contractor, 54, 113
Owen, Henry, 51–2, 96
Owen Glendower Institute,
     Machynlleth, 77

Oxford University
    All Souls College, 95, 99
    professor of political theory and
        institutions, see Adams,
        W. G. S.

Palmer, A. N., 62
Pantannas Estate, 117
Panteg
    steel works, 74
    urban district council, 74
Parliament, 19–20, 61
Payton, Walter G., 39, 58, 106
Pembroke and Haverfordwest
    constituency, 51–2
Pembrokeshire, 51–2
Penarth library, 2–3, 29, 43, 47, 48,
    56–7, 59, 68, 96, 114, 133
Pennant, Thomas, 62
Pennsylvania, 7–8, 25, 28, 82, 92
Pennsylvania Railroad Company, 7
Penrhiwceiber, 77
Penrhyn, Lord, 22, 67, 68, 107
Penrice Castle Estate, 45–6
Penydarren library, 2–3, 49, 66, 114
Philipps, John Wynford, MP, 51–2
Philipps, Owen, MP, 51–2
Phipps, H. H., of Carnegie Steel Trust,
    108–9
Pittsburgh, 7, 16, 25, 27, 92
    eisteddfod, 28, 92
    library, 16
    St David's Society, 28
Platt, Col. Henry, CB, 67
Plymouth, earl of, see Windsor
Pontarddulais, 78
Pontnewynydd, 74–5
Pontymoile, 74
Pontypool
    hospital, 96
    library, 2–3, 41, 48, 52–3, 75, 115,
        134

literary institute, 47
town, 47
town hall, 47
urban district council, 47
West Monmouthshire School, 96
Pontypridd, 54, 77
    library, 20–1, 77
    literary institute, 20
Port Dinorwic
    Shiloh Chapel, 83
    Wesleyan Chapel, 83
Porter and Hunter, architects, 54, 111
Powell Dyffryn Company, 77
Powysland Club, museum and library,
    22
Price Bros, Messrs, of Cardiff,
    contractor, 54, 110, 116
Price and Morgan, Messrs,
    contractors, 108
Public Libraries Acts, 11, 14, 20–3,
    29–30, 43, 45–8, 51, 71, 74, 77–8,
    85–7, 91
Pwllheli Liberal Club, 98

Randall, John, 108
Read, C. H., of Newport, contractor,
    116
Rees, J. Cook, of Neath, architect, 116
Rendel, Lord, 81, 101
Rhondda urban district council, 87
Rhyl
    library, 2–3, 27, 30, 44, 61, 65, 65–6,
        98, 115
    town hall, 44, 115
    town surveyor, see Goodall, A. A.
    urban district council, 115; see also
        Jones, J. W.
Richards, Edward Windsor, 29, 46
Risca Primitive Methodist Church, 83
'Robber Barons', 14
Roberts, John Herbert, MP, 65, 111
Roberts, T. F., 64

Rogerstone
    library, 2–3, 29, 41, 46, 52–3, 71,
        116, *135*
    parish council, 46, 93
Roweley, Robert, of Gresford,
    contractor, 118–19
Royal Commission on the Ancient
    and Historical Monuments of
    Scotland, 4
Royal Commission on the Ancient
    and Historical Monuments of
    Wales, 4
Royal Institution of South Wales
    library, 22
Ruskin, John, 1
Russell, S. B., architect, 58

St Andrews University, 81
St David's, bishop of, 63
Schools, Chief Inspector of, in Wales,
    68
Scotland, 4, 8, 16, 27, 33, 52, 81–2, 90
    libraries, 4, 91
    see also Dunfermline, Edinburgh
Scott, Thomas, 7
Seycelles library, 23
Shakespeare, William, 25
Shrewsbury, 39
Skewen (or Coedffranc), 63
    library, 2–3, 27, 46, 56, 63, 116, *136*
Skibo Castle and Estate, Sutherland, 8,
    27, 33–4, 66, 77–8, 82, 94, 96, 98
Slate-quarrying, 41
Smith, Henry, of Wolverley, contractor,
    39, 94, 106
Smithsonian Institution, Washington,
    9, 62, 98
Snell, H., architect, 114
Society of British Architects, 39, 53, 58
Somme, Battle of (1916), 99
South Africa, 33, 62
    libraries, 23

Speir and Beavan, architects, 52–3,
    109, 115
Spencer, Earl, 28
Staffordshire county library, 85
Steiner, George, 1
Storye, W. J. P., 65–6, 115
Stowe, Harriet Beecher, 62
Swansea
    Bible Christian Chapel, 83
    branch libraries, 72–3, 100
    central library, 20–1, 72–3
    town council, 73
Swash and Bain, of Newport,
    architects, 52–3, 116
Swedenborgian Church, 82

Taff Valley, 56
Tai-bach library, 2–4, 41, 45–6, 54, 56,
    97–8, 116–17
Talbot, Emily, 45–6, 95, 116–17
Talbot Estate, *see* Margam
Tennant, Winifred Coombe, 46, 116
Tennant Estate, 46, 116
Thomas, Arthur Llewellyn, architect,
    54, 110
Thomas, D. Alfred, MP, 27, 49, 63, 66,
    110, 112, 114, 117
Thomas, Llewelyn, JP, 108
Thomas, P. J., of Bridgend, architect,
    108
Thomas, Councillor Samuel, 114
Thomas, Sidney Gilchrist, 27, 29, 46,
    49, 92
Tinplate industry, 47
Tourism, 41, 45, 54
Trecynon library and public hall, 2–3,
    27, 29, 62, 66, 71, 117, *137*
Tredegar, 73–4, 100
    Bedwellty Park, 100
    Temperance Society, 73–4, 100
    workmen's institute and library,
        73–4, 100

Tredegar, Lord, 46, 95, 100, 116
Trefechan, 39, 106
Treharris
    library, 2–4, 38, 49, *50*, 53 55, 57,
        78, 117, *138*
    workmen's library, 78
Troedyrhiw library, 2–4, 49, 56, 58, 105,
    118
Turner and Sons, Messrs, of Cardiff,
    contractor, 114

United States of America, 12, 23, 84
United States Steel Corporation, 8, 23
University College of North Wales, 81;
    see also Bangor
University of South Wales and
    Monmouthshire, Cardiff, 81
University College of Wales,
    Aberystwyth, 64, 81–2
University of Wales, 66, 81

Varteg, 74–5
Vaughan, E. M. Bruce, architect, 53,
    109
Victoria, Queen
    Diamond Jubilee (1897), 20, 78
Vivian and Sons, industrialists, 73

Wadbrook, Mr, of Abergavenny,
    businessman, 63
Ward, C. F., of Newport, architect, 114
Warmington, Mr, of Swansea Market,
    83
Watt, James, engineer, 42–3
Welsh, Irvine, 5
Welshpool, 22
Wentsland, manor of, 47
Westminster, duke of, 22

Whitchurch
    library, 2–3, *37*, 63, 118, *138*
    parish council, 118
    war memorial, *138*
Whitfield, Louise, *see* Carnegie, Andrew
Wilkinson, John, ironmaster, 42–3
Williams, Enoch, and Sons, of
    Dowlais, contractor, 105, 113
Williams, J. H., contractor, 54, 114
Williams, R. and S., of Cardiff,
    architects, 118
Williams, Alderman Thomas, JP, of
    Gwaelod-y-garth, 114
Williams, Sir Thomas Marchaunt, 68
Williams, Major W., 68, 106
Williams, Watkin, contractor, 53, 107
Willink, W. E., architect, 52
Wilson, Andrew, *50*, 117
Windsor, Lord, of St Fagans, 29–30,
    47–9, 66, 68, 84, 107, 114, 117–18;
    see also Plymouth, earl of
Windsor Estate, architect of, *see*
    Snell, H.
Wingfield and Mackintosh Estate, 44,
    49, 105
Wolverley, near Kidderminster, 39
Women's suffrage, 46
Wrexham, 42–3, 62, 94
    borough council, 118–19
    Congregational Church, 82–3
    library, 2–4, 41, 43–4, 52, 55, 59, 64,
        66, 99, 118–19, *139*
    mayoress, 118; *see also* Evans,
        Mrs B.
    museum, 62
    town hall, 44

Ynysybwl, 77

List of Illustrations

p. 6: Anarchists and trade unionists with the now traditional black flag, 'A' symbol, and red-and-black anarcho-syndicalist banner. Photo courtesy of Freedom Press.

p. 24: A workshop of collectivized leatherworkers and harness-makers in Republican Spain, 1937.

p. 56: 'Beauty is in the street' — an image from the street actions in Paris in May 1968.

p. 80: Class War at an anti-war march in London in autumn 2002, adding vivacity to a strong political message.

p. 120: The links between punk and anarchism made graphic, in an illustration by Clifford Harper (from his 1987 book *Anarchy: A Graphic Guide*). Reproduced courtesy of Clifford Harper.

p. 148: A tear-gas canister returned to sender in the anti-globalization protests during the Summit of the Americas in Québec City, April 2001.